Great Gardens
of Britain

Great Gardens of Britain

Helena Attlee

Photographs by Alex Ramsay

F

FRANCES LINCOLN LIMITED
PUBLISHERS

Frances Lincoln Limited
4 Torriano Mews
Torriano Avenue
London NW5 2RZ
www.franceslincoln.com

British Library Cataloguing in
Publication Data
A catalogue record for this book is
available from the British Library.

ISBN 978-0-7112-3134-4

Printed and bound in China

9 8 7 6 5 4 3 2 1

HALF-TITLE PAGE Tulips in the Barn
Garden at Great Dixter.
TITLE PAGE The seventeenth-century
Topiary Garden at Levens Hall in
Cumbria.
RIGHT A view across the cornfield at
East Ruston Old Vicarage towards
Happisburgh church.

contents

CRATHES

CRARAE

LITTLE SPARTA

ALNWICK

THE GARDEN OF COSMIC SPECULATION

MOUNT
STEWART

LEVENS
HALL

SCAMPSTON

BODNANT

EAST RUSTON

POWIS CASTLE

BETH CHATTO
GARDENS

HIDCOTE

KEW GARDENS

WISLEY

SISSINGHURST

STOURHEAD

GREAT DIXTER

THE EDEN PROJECT

TRESCO

Introduction

How to choose? That's the question. How do you select only twenty from the extraordinary number of outstanding gardens in Britain? In a country where nearly four thousand gardens open their gates to the public at least once a year, it's not a task for the faint hearted.

It is quite common to see gardens planted in the 'English' style abroad, but it is only by looking at gardens across the length and breadth of Britain, as we have done, that you realize how diverse that style really is. *Great Gardens of Britain* is a celebration of diversity.

Britain offers the gardener a range of different climates, and this contributes greatly to the diversity of the country's gardens. There are gardens in this book from the west coast, where the Gulf Stream softens the climate and increases rainfall, making it possible in some places to grow tender plants from all over the world. At Mount Stewart in Northern Ireland, for example, the garden lies on a salt-water lough, not far from the Irish Sea and the Gulf Stream. These features combine to create a climate so mild that tender Mexican lilies (*Beschorneria yuccoides*), *Puya alpestris*, and the extraordinary Lobster Claw (*Clianthus puniceus*) from New Zealand thrive in the Mount Stewart gardens. What could be more different from this than the parched gardens of the East Anglian flatlands? At East Ruston, on Norfolk's windswept North Sea coast, agaves, aloes, dasylirion and cacti grow in the Desert Wash, a garden of shattered rocks and water-gouged gullies, designed to resemble parts of the Arizona desert, while Beth Chatto's Mediterranean Gravel Garden thrives in the driest climate in Britain.

Great Gardens of Britain also encompasses a range of diverse settings. Some gardens have been made in unlikely and difficult places, like Little Sparta high among the Pentland Hills in Scotland, and the Abbey Gardens on Tresco, a small, windswept island 30 miles off the Cornish coast. Others, such as Sissinghurst in the Weald of Kent, are set in a gentler and more sheltered landscape.

Gardening has been an important part of British culture for hundreds of years, and *Great Gardens of Britain* encompasses an enormous range of styles from many different periods. The oldest gardens in the book are Powis Castle, one of the few examples of an Italianate, baroque, terraced garden to survive in Britain, and Levens Hall in Cumbria. Both were made in the late seventeenth century, and both are dominated by the toppling forms of ancient topiary. The English landscape movement is represented in the serene and infinitely beautiful garden of Stourhead in Wiltshire, where Henry Hoare II dammed the river below his house to make a lake, and furnished the surrounding landscape with classical buildings. There are Victorian and Edwardian gardens, gardens in the Arts and Crafts style, and others built between the wars. Among the examples of contemporary style are Scampston in North Yorkshire, with fashionable perennial planting was designed by Piet Oudolf, and Charles Jencks' sensational landforms in the Garden of Cosmic Speculation on the Scottish borders. The twenty-first century is represented here by gardens that have changed the nature of garden visiting, attracting the attention of a whole new sector of the public. At the Alnwick Garden the Duchess of Northumberland's crowd-pulling water garden is heaven on earth for children, and Tim Smit's Eden Project in Cornwall educates and entertains over a million visitors every year. Education is also the theme at Wisley, the Royal Horticultural Society's flagship garden, devoted to ensuring that Britain's long tradition of horticulture continues to flourish at both an amateur and a professional level. Kew Gardens, the world's greatest centre for horticultural research, is also included. The stories of many of the gardens in the book are inevitably bound up with the lives of some of the greatest figures in British horticultural history, people like Christopher Lloyd, Vita Sackville West and Lawrence Johnston.

Great Gardens of Britain is no place for obscure or lesser-known gardens. It celebrates gardens whose excellence has made them famous all over the world.

Crarae

At Crarae you will find one of Britain's finest collections of rhododendrons, azaleas, magnolias and conifers set in the wonderful Highland landscape that surrounds Loch Fyne. It is a family garden, a place created, extended and nurtured by three generations of the Campbells. Grace, Lady Campbell, began work in 1912. The site of her new garden was a steep wooded ravine with a fast-flowing burn tumbling through it towards the loch. The soil was acid and the air mild and damp. She is thought to have looked to her nephew Reginald Farrer, the most adventurous plant hunter of his generation, for advice on the new garden. Farrer's influence is evident both in the international palette of plants that grow at Crarae and in the naturalistic style of planting. His expeditions took him to the remotest parts of China, Japan and the Himalayas, and it seems likely that he would have alerted his aunt to the similarities between the conditions in her Scottish glen and those in the Himalayan gorges where he had made some of his most exciting botanical discoveries. Lady Campbell, her son Sir George Campbell and her grandson Sir Ilay Campbell filled the spaces between the trees in the ravine with treasures brought back by plant hunters from China, Nepal and Tibet, or given to them by gardening friends from all over Scotland. One such example is the *Rhododendron* 'Mrs James Horlicks', given to Lady Campbell by the inventor of the eponymous milky drink, who gardened near Kintyre. The garden grew slowly and steadily, extending through the natural woodland on the steep hillside until it eventually covered 20 hectares/50 acres. Lady Campbell

ABOVE The Campbell family home stands beside the burn at Crarae.
LEFT Sir George amassed a collection of *Sorbus*, the mountain ash, from all over the world. This *Sorbus hupehensis* is native to north-west China. It bears its pink berries against the blazing backdrop of maples in full colour.

planted hundreds of rhododendrons, and Sir George imported rare conifers from all over the temperate world, using them to create a dark backdrop for the vibrant colours of the rhododendron flowers. He built up a varied collection of eucalyptus and of nothofagus, or southern beech, a small genus of highly ornamental and fast-growing trees which originated over 80 million years ago in the southern hemisphere. Nine different sorts of nothofagus grow in Chile and Argentina, and Crarae holds the National Collection. The garden is also planted for spectacular autumn colour, with stands of maples and berry-covered rowans from all over the world.

Sir George Campbell never went on plant-hunting expeditions himself, but concentrated his energies on extending the garden into the wild and rocky landscape that surrounded it. He is said to have made a habit of scaling rock faces in order to establish young plants in their new homes, often putting the plant, together with a handful of earth, into the pocket of his jacket, leaving his hands free for climbing. At the head of the valley, beyond the garden boundary, Sir George established experimental plantations of imported trees such as redwood, sequoia, spruce and hemlock, to see if any of them might be grown commercially in Scotland in the future. He planted yet more rhododendrons between the trees. The Second World War put a stop to the experiment, but in 1956 some of the land was given to the Forestry Commission. The remaining plantation will be the focus of an important new phase, the restoration project that has been underway since 2001, when Crarae was taken over by the National Trust for Scotland. For over twenty years, the garden had been managed by the Crarae Garden Charitable Trust, to which Sir Ilay Campbell gifted it in 1978. Since taking over, the Trust has worked hard to restore the complex infrastructure of bridges, steps and paths. The planting has been enriched with many new rhododendrons collected from the wild.

On a fine day in May, Loch Fyne is unruffled, a vast mirror that fills Crarae with soft, bright light. The garden is in the grip of spring. The burn is full of sparkling water, and on its banks gunnera and the glossy leaves of yellow skunk cabbage (*Lysichiton americanus*) burst from bare earth. Bright pink candelabra primulas, hostas and the blowsiest, bluest meconopsis thrive in the damp ground. This is the climax of Crarae's year, the month that sees 600 different varieties of rhododendron stain the sides of the ravine with pools of vivid pink, red, mauve, yellow and startling white. They make flowering arches across paths, and crowd the edges of narrow streams that cut through the mossy ground. The steep slope gives the rhododendrons extra height, adding drama to the view. The air is full of the sound of water clattering

The pink flush in the trunk of a stand of Scots pines chimes with the mauve of a rhododendron that flowers beside them.

over stones, and of the thick, honeyed scent of *R. luteum*. The garden is full of surprises. Narrow, enticing paths flank the burn and push deep into the woods, where bluebells, primroses, wood anemones and violets flower on mossy ground. The damp air encourages moss, and the contours of every plant and tree are concealed beneath a shaggy green coat. You never know what will be around the next corner. It might be a Chilean flame tree (*Embrothium coccineum*), blazing with orange flowers, an apple-blossom-pink cascade of rhododendron flowers set against the lime-green leaves of a beech tree or the football-sized flowers of *Rhododendron* 'Sinogrande'. The garden is alive with birds. There are otters in the burn and red squirrels in the woods. Sit still, and a deer may trot out of the trees, pause to consider you, and trot quietly on.

Crathes Castle

Crathes Castle is a magnificent building, a great stark tower built between 1553 and 1596 by the Burnetts, who had lived in the area since 1323. Turrets, chimneys and gables soften its profile, and it is covered in a soft pink harling that entirely undermines its austerity. The garden covers nearly 1.6 hectares/4 acres of ground below the castle. On the upper terraces, closest to the castle, yew topiary was planted by Sir Thomas Burnett at the beginning of the eighteenth century. Yew hedges were added to the layout in the late eighteenth and early nineteenth centuries. By the end of the nineteenth century fruit and vegetables were grown only in the Lower Walled Garden, and the upper terraces were entirely ornamental. Gertrude Jekyll wrote a flattering description of the Crathes flower borders at the end of the nineteenth century in *Some English Gardens* (1904). However, the garden's appearance today dates only from the first half of the twentieth century, when Sir James Burnett and his wife, Sybil, worked the existing features into a fascinating and densely woven fabric of garden rooms and long vistas lined with Lady Burnett's magnificent herbaceous borders. Sir James's fascination for rare and exotic trees added another layer of interest in the garden. The Burnett family had lived at Crathes for 400 years by 1951, when Sir James made over the castle and part of the estate to the National Trust for Scotland.

Sometimes the Lower Walled Garden at Crathes conceals the castle. Sometimes it reveals it, at the far end of a colourful double border perhaps, perfectly framed by topiary, or glimpsed suggestively between trees and shrubs. For the first-time visitor, this part of the garden is a maze, a wonderful confusion of paths and densely planted rooms. Sooner or later, everyone finds their way to the centre of the puzzle, where an ancient Portuguese laurel (*Prunus lusitanica*) grows, its trunk knotted,

FAR LEFT Crathes Castle on a misty morning in September.
LEFT A view along double herbaceous borders in the Lower Walled Garden is stopped by an ancient Portuguese laurel at the garden's centre. The planting in the beds still reflects Sybil Burnett's preference for strong primary colours, and the borders blaze with colour from June to October.
BELOW The Gold Garden was developed by the Trust after Lady Burnett's death. They were assisted by the late Frances Chenevix Trench, who had worked alongside Lady Burnett on many occasions.
BOTTOM Late afternoon sun ignites the colours of the dense planting in the upper terraces. Many of the varieties of plants at Crathes are no longer commercially available, and this makes their preservation here all the more important.
PAGES 16–17 The Fountain Garden, where the parterres are packed with flowers of every shade of blue. The magnificent hedges that fill the horizon are undergoing radical restoration.

split and partially eviscerated. The tree's branches have been pruned for hundreds of years into a perfect dome. This gives it the appearance of a giant peg, the king-pin around which the garden revolves. Four paths radiate from it, each one lined by borders. Lady Burnett's principal interest was in herbaceous planting, and in these borders and the rooms that lead off them, her plantsmanship is still evident. She planted boldly, creating unusual colour combinations, and building up collections of several different varieties of the same species. In spring, the air over the White Border is saturated with the scent of a magnificent collection of philadelphus, and in late summer white hydrangeas dominate the show. The planting in the double herbaceous border is dense and intensely coloured, and at its far end are the tower and turrets of the castle, a flag flying against the clear blue evening sky, and a weathercock glinting in the last rays of the sunlight.

Each room in the Lower Walled Garden comes into its own at different times of the year, but in the Golden Garden, time of day is almost as important as season. Go there on a summer evening, just after the sun has dipped behind the trees. The air cools suddenly, dew begins to rise, but the garden glows in the twilight, as if radiating stored heat. Only then will you fully appreciate the effect that Lady Burnett hoped to achieve. She had always wanted to make a gold garden of the kind described by Gertrude Jekyll in *Colour Schemes for the Flower Garden*. Sadly, however, she died before the garden could be realized. In 1973 the National Trust for Scotland planted the Golden Garden to her original plans. Golden cypress, holly, laburnum and elder create a radiant backdrop for beds packed with 'Golden Apeldoorn' tulips in spring, with Bowles' golden grass, the golden currant (*Ribes sanguineum* 'Brocklebankii'), *Berberis thunbergii* 'Aurea', yellow snapdragons, rock roses, day lilies and golden hops, all of them gathered round the *Acer cappadocicum* 'Aureum' that will blaze gold in autumn.

One of Crarae's great delights is a series of glasshouses set against the retaining wall of the Rose Garden. They were built in 1886 to a cutting-edge design by Mackenzie and Moncur, and thoroughly renovated in 1976. Inside, the National Collection of dianthus fills the air with a spicy scent. Next door the stepped staging is crammed with a highly ornamental display of pelargoniums, begonias, fuchsias and canna lilies. A magnificent vine covered in black grapes grows against the wall. In the flower bed outside, the pale spires of the summer hyacinth (*Galtonia candicans*) push up through a fiery carpet of dahlias.

Steps link the Lower Walled Garden to the upper terraces, where Lady Burnett filled in the existing structure of ancient yew hedges with the Rose Garden, the Fountain Garden and the Upper Pool Garden.

LEFT, ABOVE In the upper terraces the triangular beds of the Rose Garden are filled with red, pink and white floribunda and hybrid tea roses.
LEFT, BELOW The planting in the Lower Walled Garden's West Border is restricted to herbaceous plants with pale blue or pink flowers.
RIGHT The glowing late summer border in the Upper Pool Garden is Lady Burnett's greatest achievement.

The croquet lawn on the first terrace was probably created in the mid-nineteenth century, when the game first became fashionable. The immaculate expanse of turf is dominated by the castle. The formal atmosphere of this simple space is only undermined by two vast and delightful topiary forms that topple into a messy embrace above the gate.

Despite persistent pruning, the hedges that surround the Rose and Fountain Gardens had by 2001 become too big. Since then they have been severely pruned, and then carefully mulched, watered and fed to promote regeneration. In places, a skeleton of pale branches is still exposed to the light. Inside the hedges, parterre beds surround an Italianate fountain. Each is packed with flowers of a different shade of blue, as if filled by the evening sky. There are the dusky blues of catmint and perovskia, and the brighter ones of *Echium vulgare* 'Blue Bedder' and a vibrant cranesbill geranium.

The topmost terrace, immediately below the castle, is occupied by the Upper Pool Garden. This is Lady Burnett's *pièce de résistance*, a wonderfully clean and simple design of interlocking beds set around a square lily pond. L-shaped cornerstones of yew around the pool make it impossible to see the whole of the garden at once from ground level. However, Lady Burnett originally designed the layout to be enjoyed from the drawing room in the Victorian extension to the castle. The extension was destroyed by a fire, but the view can now be seen from a small terrace beside the castle. It is a late summer garden, and in August the two glorious Chilean leatherwoods (*Eucryphia glutinosa*) that grow over the wall are smothered in pale blossom. The beds against the wall are packed with a magnificent combination of red, gold and bronze flowers. There are rock roses, crocosmias, kniphofia, dahlias and swathes of achillea. The grass is velvety, the topiary perfectly clipped, and the beds seem to absorb and radiate the saturated gold of evening light.

The Garden of Cosmic Speculation

Something starts to happen as soon as you enter the drive at Portrack. You will notice the undulating line of the hedges to either side of you, and even at this early stage you may suspect that you are seeing something more than a demonstration of expert pruning. Then, at the bottom of a short descent, the hedges give way to a drystone wall with the same rolling profile. The wall is so unusual and so exquisitely made that you will need to stop the car, get out and examine it. But this is all supposing that you have managed to reach Portrack House at all, and that you have gained permission to visit Charles Jencks' and the late Maggie Keswick's Garden of Cosmic

Speculation. For this garden is, in Jencks' own words, 'open to the public, but not easily'. So why should you navigate the lanes on the one open day a year, or seek written permission to visit on another occasion? Because this is one of the most exciting, intellectually demanding and aesthetically challenging gardens of our time.

Jencks and Keswick began to make a new landscape around the Keswick family's home in 1988. They worked on it together until Maggie Keswick's untimely death from cancer in 1995. Since then Charles Jencks has continued to develop the landscape, using landforms and other structures to celebrate ideas about nature and

The undulating Worm Hedge lines the drive below Portrack House, leading to the garden.

20

the cosmos, and to explore new discoveries in science. It may seem revolutionary to use a landscape as a vehicle for expressing and exploring ideas, but Jencks has done nothing new. He would be the first to acknowledge that the garden architects of Renaissance Italy worked closely with iconographers to encode their gardens with messages about politics, philosophy or the moral stature of their patrons. In the sixteenth century every educated person was familiar with the stories of classical mythology, and for the garden iconographer myths and pastoral poems became the source of a universal visual language that was expressed through statues, fountains and buildings.

Science replaces mythology as a visual language in the Garden of Cosmic Speculation. Jencks sees the garden as 'a celebration of science that we are the first generation to know'. Mythology was once a universal language, but science is not. Jencks is well aware of this. 'Many of us remain blind to [scientific] discoveries', he says, 'because they are not reinterpreted at a cultural level and given artistic expression.' Jencks has tried to meet this challenge in the garden, but visitors must work hard to understand the 'new grammar of landscape design' that he and Keswick have developed. The triumph of the Garden of Cosmic Speculation is that it works for the non-scientist, for Jencks has tapped into a rich and powerful source of new images and shapes. Nobody can fail to admire the garden's beauty, or Jencks' wit, and nor can they leave it without knowing a little more about biology, cosmology and physics.

This highly intellectual garden had a very practical beginning. It all started when Maggie Keswick decided that the couple's two children needed a place to swim. She and Jencks excavated a small stream and bog to make a swimming place, discovering in the process that they could mould the excavated soil into any shape they chose. The diggers were called in again to create the lakes and landforms that form the core of the garden. Maggie Keswick designed two interlocking lakes, and Jencks created the sculpted earthworks that enclose them. Keswick was an expert in Chinese garden history. She knew that Chinese gardens often reproduce the natural landscape in a miniaturized and idealized form, and she looked to the rolling Dumfriesshire landscape that surrounds Portrack for inspiration. Jencks' extraordinary landforms were also inspired by the natural landscape. Even at this early stage, however, he was looking for a metaphor that could be used throughout the garden, and he found it in the snaking curves – or waveforms – of the surrounding hills. Jencks recognizes waveforms as one of the fundamental structures of life, naming brain, sound, light and water waves as a few examples

to prove his point. The undulating Worm Hedge and the walls that flank the drive are the first glimpses of the waveforms that are repeated in the seven red Chinese bridges beyond the lakes. Soliton waves, which retain their shape and energy over long distances, have inspired the design of a series of wrought-iron gates all over the garden. The magnificent stone ha-ha that separates the garden from the fields is made from overlapping waveforms, designed to show how energy waves travel through each other.

The Snail Mound and the Snake Mound – the landforms that wrap around Maggie Keswick's lakes – were Jencks' first experiment in waveform structures. They repeat the shapes of the distant hills, but in this miniaturized form the waves are perfected and their impact more intense. The view from the top of the Snake Mound is across the two peat-brown lakes, the lovely curled peninsula and the grassy causeway that divides them. A small blue rowing boat is moored beneath cherry trees. At the end of a midsummer day the sun lingers late into evening. Low light casts deep shadows across the body of Jencks' sinuous snake, sharpening and defining the twists and folds of its contours. Nothing in this view is unmeditated, nothing unintentional. It has the atmosphere of an ancient, sacred site.

Only the oystercatchers break the silence on this quiet evening, until a goods train suddenly roars along the garden boundary, drawing attention to the Garden of the Worthies that Jencks has built beside the track. When North-West Rail decided to demolish the bridge that spans the River Nith next to the garden, Jencks insisted on designing a handsome replacement. He also took possession of the old structure and cut it into eighteen parts. Each part became a carriage for a figure from Scottish history that Jencks considered

The graceful curve of the Snake Mound leads the eye across Maggie Keswick's 'slug lakes' to the double helix of the Snail Mound.

LEFT The 'carriage' dedicated to the philanthropist Andrew Carnegie, one of many famous Scots represented in Jencks' Garden of the Worthies.
BELOW The railway bridge that Jencks designed on the garden's edge echoes the shape of the distant hills and the curving wave forms found throughout the garden.
RIGHT The metal banners that hang from a line of poplar trees below the railway line mark notable incidents and figures from Scottish history.

worthy of celebration. The worthies are pulled along by their own train. Each has a nameplate that is also engraved with a quotation. Jencks gives visitors to the garden an opportunity to have their own train-driving experience. First they must navigate a path narrow enough to pass between the buttocks of a magnificent earthwork. Out in the open again, the rails recede into the distance, carrying the visitors out across the river to a miniature version of the new bridge. Passengers on the real railway are carried across the bridge and into

the distance, but Jencks' visitors are left behind to watch the sand martins busy with their nests in the riverbank.

At first glance, the Physic Garden with its box-lined beds might appear quite traditional. But that impression falls away as soon as you notice aluminium sculptures of the double helix, an ear, a nose, fingers and lips. This part of the garden celebrates both the human senses and discoveries in biology about the evolution of DNA. Each box-lined parterre represents a cell. In one there is an aluminium

LEFT, ABOVE In the Physic Garden a pair of lips hangs suspended from a model of DNA's double helix to represent the sense of taste. The lovely undulating contours of the Dragon Wall can be seen beyond the box parterres.
LEFT, BELOW The branching steps of the Universe Cascade represent the crucial developmental 'jumps' that make up the history of the universe.
RIGHT, ABOVE The Black Hole Terrace shows the distortions of space and time caused by extreme gravity. Jencks describes the wood in the background as 'a place of illusions, tricks and confusions' and he has christened that part of the garden 'Taking Leave of Your Senses'.
RIGHT, BELOW Inscriptions abound in the garden. Here they appear on a path made of black and white plastic piping that winds through a grove of silver birch trees.

hand beneath the double helix. Thistles, nettles and docks grow around it, leaving no doubt that this is the sense of touch. Near by, a pair of lips is surrounded by wild strawberries, and an ear swings in the breeze. A grass tump in the shape of a double helix has an eye in its crown. Only the sixth sense is entirely unexpected. It is intuition, the female sense. A woman observes the brain that she holds in her antennae-like fingers. Verbascums seem intent on appearing intuitive, too, and they crane their heavy heads inquisitively around the curves of the double helix.

The Garden of Cosmic Speculation is designed to challenge the 'mechanistic metaphors that underlie modern science', and the Universe Cascade that tumbles down the steep hill between Portrack House and the Physic Garden is Jencks' protest against Big Bang theory. 'Whatever its cause,' he says, 'it is not a big bang since it is infinitely small, hot, fast-moving . . . ' His vision is of a universe that unfolds in a series of jumps – or steps – down the hillside. Each part of the cascade represents an evolutionary breakthrough.

Do you want to look at the universe from another perspective? If so, go to the Symmetry Break Terrace outside the house, where a pattern of grass and gravel represents critical advances in its evolution. While you are up there, why not allow gravity to pull you into the Black Hole Terrace? And don't forget the brushed aluminium Comet Bridge, where Jencks eats picnics, or the Quark Walk. There is always more to see and more to learn from this extraordinary landscape.

EXTERMINISMS
WORDS THAT KILL

Little Sparta

The track that links Little Sparta to the road is long and rough. To either side of it curlews and gulls soar over the broad open landscape of the Pentland Hills. Stonypath, the small cottage at the top of the track, was home to Ian Hamilton Finlay, poet and artist, from 1966 until his death in 2006. During the early years Hamilton Finlay and his partner, Sue Swan, devoted themselves to transforming the derelict cottage and the windswept farmyard beyond it into a comfortable place to live with their young children. They planted trees for shelter, laid paths, transplanted wild flowers, and dug out the pond in the yard and a lochan, or small loch, on the hillside.

Hamilton Finlay was already a poet by the time they moved to Stonypath. He wrote what is known as concrete poetry, a style that gives as much weight to the typographical arrangement of words as to their meaning. The garden that developed around the cottage and in the old farmyard was a natural extension of his poetry, a three-dimensional poem, complex, many-layered and multi-faceted. It is Hamilton Finlay's intellect made visible, and it is also a series of contrasting garden landscapes, large and small, open and enclosed, that sit comfortably together in the larger landscape of the Pentland Hills. Words are everywhere, beautifully cut, carved or painted on plinths, plaques, benches, bridges, tree columns, gates, arches, urns and obelisks. Hamilton Finlay worked like the court humanists of Renaissance Italy, commissioning artists and craftsmen of the highest calibre to realize his designs in wood, stone and metal. In 1980 he renamed the garden Little Sparta to commemorate the bitter disputes that he had first with the Scottish Arts Council and then with Strathclyde Regional Council. He always referred to these battles as the Little Spartan Wars.

The Little Sparta Trust has published a small guide to the garden for visitors. Don't doubt that you need it. Memorial plaques to sunk ships and images of aircraft carriers, tanks, grenades and machine guns might alert you to the theme of conflict, and when you see 'Liberty', 'Equality', 'Eternity' and the date 1793 carved into pillars in the Temple Pool Garden you are bound to think of the French Revolution. But how detailed is your knowledge of philosophy, one of Hamilton Finlay's themes, or of classical mythology? Will you recognize Philemon's and Baucis' cottage? They were the old couple in Ovid's *Metamorphoses* who unwittingly sheltered Jupiter and Mercury when

The rising sun picks out a quotation from the eighteenth-century French thinker and revolutionary Saint-Just. In the background are Lochan Eck and the Pentland Hills.

LEFT The cottage of Baucis and Philemon reflected in the Temple Pool. A single golden slate suggests the splendid shrine it will become.

RIGHT, ABOVE Hamilton Finlay transformed a simple barn into this Temple of Apollo. His children used to sail their boats on the pool in the foreground.

RIGHT, BELOW The gigantic gilded head of Apollo gazes blindly at the visitor from trees that border the Upper Pool. It was modelled on a portrait of Saint-Just.

they were travelling in disguise. As a reward, the gods transformed their shabby cottage into a golden temple. Hamilton Finlay chose to capture the cottage in metamorphosis, and if you know what you are looking for, you will notice a single golden slate on its roof. The lintel above the door is changing too. One half of it is beautifully smooth, and the other half is made from roughly hewn stone. Hamilton Finlay transformed the barn on the opposite side of the yard into a temple dedicated in an inscription above doors and windows to 'Apollo, His Music, His Missiles, His Muses'. He painted classical columns

on the façade and around the door. Apollo, guardian of the arts, skilful archer and god of harmony, is the spirit of the garden, and the temple is his shrine. You may come across his golden head among the fallen leaves in the Wild Garden. Here, he is identified as 'Apollo terroriste'. All of these are serious themes, but you must also be ready for Hamilton Finlay's jokes. In the small front garden, for example, a stone set among a group of sycamores is inscribed with the words 'Bring back the birch'. A small birch tree grows immediately behind it. His wit is everywhere. A stile links the Wild Garden to the Lochan Eck Garden. The words beautifully carved into the wood of a post on one side read 'THESIS *fence*. ANTITHESIS *gate'*, and on the other side 'SYNTHESIS *stile*' is carved.

Everything in this garden is well made, and in the woods beyond the temple a beautifully proportioned brick path snakes between trees. In places the bricks are imprinted with the tree names. A fawn and a nymph dance in dappled sunlight. A stone column is inscribed with words from Virgil's *Georgics*: '*Fortu natus et ille deos qui novit*' (Happy is he who also knows the woodland gods). And happy is he who also knows Latin, you might think, grasping your guidebook ever more tightly. A good knowledge of landscape painters working in Italy in the seventeenth century would help too, as their initials, monograms or nicknames are carved into stones and tree plaques all over this part of the garden. The iconography is densely written here, among the trees and pools. Wordplay is constant, sometimes poetic, sometimes aggressive, and always closely connected to its setting. A stone by the water in the Wild Garden reads:

THE SHADY GROVE
THE MURMURING STREAM
THE SHADY STREAM
THE MURMURING GROVE

The Lochan Eck Garden is open and boggy, a heather-covered space on the edge of grazing land. Here Hamilton Finlay's poetry is sparser and built on a larger scale to suit the hills that surround it. Three short stone walls are set one above the other on the hillside, each one divided in two by the path. The first is inscribed with the words 'LITTLE FIELDS LONG HORIZONS'. Then comes 'LITTLE FIELDS LONG FOR HORIZONS', and finally 'HORIZONS LONG FOR LITTLE FIELDS'. A path leads along the edge of the lochan, where wild orchids grow.

OPPOSITE, ABOVE These inscriptions play on the essential nature of a stile with the wit that was typical of Hamilton Finlay.

OPPOSITE, BELOW One of three plaques on the wall of the front garden, commemorating the loss of Flower Class corvettes during the Battle of the Atlantic.

BELOW, LEFT The garden is littered with 'classical' remains. This column stands by the Temple Pool, near the entrance to the Woodland Garden.

BELOW, RIGHT Hamilton Finlay shared Saint-Just's views on classical civilization.

THE·WORLD
HAS·BEEN
EMPTY·SINCE
THE·ROMANS
SAINT·JUST

Alnwick

One day, the lawn at the entrance to the Alnwick Garden will be developed. But until then, on a fine summer afternoon the broad swathe of grass is reminiscent of the piazza in some small Italian town. People sit or lie in colourful groups on the sloping ground. They eat ice creams, share picnics and gaze at the Grand Cascade that is the hallmark and most famous feature of this brand-new British garden. Alnwick does not attract the usual garden-visiting public. These are holiday crowds, dominated by children looking for adventure among the garden fountains, labyrinth, rope bridges and tree houses. It is a garden in uproar. The sound of falling water is everywhere, and with it come the happy screams of children and the thud of tiny plastic tractors being ridden at speed across gravel. Everywhere you look, children are dressing, undressing or triumphantly wet to the skin. The atmosphere is anarchic and enormously happy. When the Duchess of Northumberland first embarked on this £42 million garden project in 1996, she had a vision of a 'place without rules', where children would be free to play in any way they chose. Mission accomplished.

There has been a garden on this site since the mid-eighteenth century. By the end of the twentieth century, however, it was derelict, and the ground had been used as a tree nursery for many years. The Duchess of Northumberland commissioned Wirtz International, the Belgian father-and-son design team of Jacques and Peter Wirtz, to create the garden. The project began in March 1996. Today the garden welcomes 800,000 visitors a year, making it second only to Kew and Wisley in popularity.

Alnwick's Grand Cascade consists of a gigantic water staircase enclosed by handsome serpentine walls made from Darney stone, a local sandstone. It is flanked to either side by snaking hornbeam tunnels. The cascade is an enormous structure, and a clever use of perspective makes it look larger still. The water tumbles down eighteen deep steps, catching the light and flicking up sparkling arcs of spray as it goes. Every half-hour the cascade explodes into a mêlée of arching jets of jewel-bright water that spring up from the sides and the centre of the cascade, crossing over and under each other to make rainbows in the sunlight. This is the moment that the children wait for, the moment when they can dash beneath the great jets that arch over the terrace at the base of the cascade. Their tiny, soaking figures appear as a moving frieze behind a curtain of water,

RIGHT Alnwick is made for children and this small visitor is captivated by the Grand Cascade.
OPPOSITE Every half-hour a different sequence of water jets springs from the Grand Cascade. At the climax of the display a great mass of water arches over the terraces, creating maximum excitement among the children who run about beneath it.

adding another layer to the cascade's magnificent performance. Single, unexpected jets as bright and powerful as fireworks bring the display to a close.

Every half-hour the cascade's computer-controlled hydraulic system produces one of four different sequences, which translates into two hours of unpredictable fun. In between displays children flock to the Serpent Garden, where twelve fountains are enclosed in the coils of a holly hedge. William Pye, one of Britain's best-known water sculptors, has designed the fountains to illustrate a series of water-related scientific principles. Favourite with the children is the Torricelli sculpture, made to illustrate hydrostatic pressure. Water rises slowly in four transparent pipes, until it is level with the surface of a pool built on high ground above the Serpent Garden. Tension rises with the water level, until suddenly a pneumatically powered valve below ground releases the hydrostatically charged water into a circle of vertical jets.

OPPOSITE This sculpture in the foreground is in the Serpent Garden. It was designed by William Pye to demonstrate the Coanda effect, which causes water to cling to the underside of smooth, overhanging surfaces, so that it appears to defy gravity.
LEFT The serpentine hornbeam tunnel that lines the Grand Cascade is made from 850 hornbeams. The trees were already ten years old when they were planted, so the tunnel made an immediate impact on the garden.
BELOW Water is led down a rill to a pool in a secluded corner of the garden.

Alnwick is a 17-hectare/42-acre garden, and it also contains quieter, more meditative spaces than those dominated by water. The hornbeam tunnels that flank the cascade turn and twist in imitation of the cascade's serpentine wall. They are filled with a green, sub-aquatic light that is a tranquil contrast to the flashing, glinting displays outside of sun on water. The hornbeams were already ten years old when the tunnel was planted, and now they entirely clothe the arching framework 6 metres/20 feet above ground.

Through a triple arch, one of the few surviving features of the original garden, lies the Ornamental Garden. This is a rectangular walled garden that Jacques and Peter Wirtz have divided and enclosed with pleached crab apples, rills, pergolas and hedges. The beds are planted with a mixture of ornamental plants and soft fruit. Currants of every known colour alternate with beds of Japanese anemones, roses and delphiniums. You might think that you are back in a traditional garden, the garden as you know it, until you come to the square pool at the centre. Late afternoon sun has taken the chill off the air, and small boys in wetsuits seem to have swimming in mind. Even here, in this more tranquil place, the water is always moving. Great aerating bubbles rise from the water at random intervals, as if the pool were inhabited by giant carp. As the crowds recede, white doves come to the rill to wash.

A long queue builds up in front of the entrance to the Poison Garden. The ornate metal gates are unlocked to admit a small group of visitors, and locked firmly behind them. No one enters this part of the garden without a guide. Inside, they learn about the dangerous properties of plants, both familiar and unfamiliar. The garden is used by the local drug education project, and among the exhibits are coca, catha, opium poppies and marijuana plants. The flame-shaped beds also contain belladonna, tobacco, wolfsbane, castor oil and mandrake plants.

Inside the Poison Garden the atmosphere may be subdued, but beyond its gates the celebratory, holiday atmosphere is undiminished. Small children ride tractors towards the base of the cascade. They fill the front loaders with water and peddle gravely off to dump it on the grass. Everyone is busy, concentrated on their own, private water-moving missions. There is no time for tears in the Alnwick Garden.

Pots filled with agapanthus in the Ornamental Garden. They stand in front of the triple arch that formed the entrance to Alnwick's original garden.

Levens Hall

LEFT A view past the Great Umbrella in the Topiary Garden to the park on the other side of the road, where black fallow deer and a small herd of Bagot goats roam freely.
BELOW The Topiary Garden used to flood only once a century. Now winter floods are a regular occurrence, covering the garden in mud. By midsummer, however, order is restored and there is no sign of the water mayhem.

Levens is particularly famous for its Topiary Garden, but that is just one element in a much larger landscape created by Guillaume Beaumont for Colonel James Grahme in c.1694. Little is known of Beaumont's life, although a portrait made of him in c.1700 bears an inscription describing him as 'Gardener to King James' and designer of gardens at 'Hampton Court Palace and Levens'. At Levens the backdrop to his design was a beautiful Elizabethan house, Levens Hall, which had accumulated around a thirteenth-century tower. Grahme enlarged the building by adding a service wing to its south side. A plan of the garden made by Robert Skyring in 1750 hangs in the great hall. It shows the same compartments divided by ancient hedges, the same tree-lined walks, miniature orchards and spacious bowling green that exist today.

Some schools pride themselves on developing their pupils' 'individuality'. If Levens Hall were such a school it would be doing its job well, and the occupants of the seventeenth-century Topiary Garden would be members of the sixth form. A vast wedding cake with five toppling layers stands next to towering umbrellas, lollipops, pyramids, cones and skinny upright trunks encircled by discs of foliage like the clipped coats of French poodles. These are the main performers, and some of them are so fat and so truly 'individual' that they block your

RIGHT, ABOVE A view along the double Pastel Borders in June, looking towards the Beech Circle. A blue and white colour scheme predominates at this time of year. The wooden pyramids at the back of the border support matched pairs of viticella clematis. The beds are mirror images of each other.

RIGHT, BELOW David Austin's English roses fill the parterre beds in the Rose Garden, to one side of the Topiary Garden.

route or jostle you off the path. At their feet are droves of smaller but equally complex topiary forms, the bizarre pieces in an unknown board game. As if this were not entertainment enough, the box-lined parterre beds are planted with a succession of striking colours throughout the year. First come the tulips, planted in blocks of a single colour to create maximum impact. One year, late summer will see some beds blazing with lemon-yellow snapdragons (*Antirrhinum majus* 'Liberty Classic Yellow') and others with the deep purple flowers of *Verbena rigida*. But who knows what will happen next? Chris Crowder, who has been head gardener since 1986, ensures that the display changes every year. At the northern end of the Topiary Garden the beds are packed with a mixture of David Austin's highly scented English roses. They are in full flower by midsummer, turning the air thick with their spicy scent, and they continue to perform until the onset of winter.

Beyond the Topiary Garden, Beaumont took his proportions from the domestic scale of the house. Nothing is very large here, yet the garden seems to unfold in an endless patchwork of beautifully planted spaces. First come the orchards, four handkerchief-sized grids of apples, quinces, medlars and plums neatly divided by paths and punctuated at the centre by a circular space. Beaumont repeated this arrangement of quadrants around a circle again and again throughout the garden.

The old fruit trees in the orchards are beautifully pruned, and in spring sheets of pillar-box red 'Apeldoorn' tulips surround their mossy trunks. Levens is a good place for trees and hedges. Everywhere you look they are trained with an attention that is almost Japanese in its intensity. The towering hedge that surrounds the Beech Circle at the centre of the garden is pruned to a lustrous smoothness that

BELOW A tracery of branches inside the great Beech Circle. The trees are thought to be three hundred years old.
RIGHT Chris Crowder gardens for maximum impact. In the Pastel Borders regular explosions of *Crambe cordifolia* are teamed up with blue delphiniums, white rosebay willowherb (*Epilobium angustifolium*), catmint, hostas, violas and *Geranium phaeum* 'Album' in midsummer.
PAGES 46–47 A view of the Pastel Borders from the bowling green. The edge of the green is marked with a dense belt of catmint (*Nepeta* 'Six Hills Giant'). Clematis and sweet peas cover the wooden pyramids.

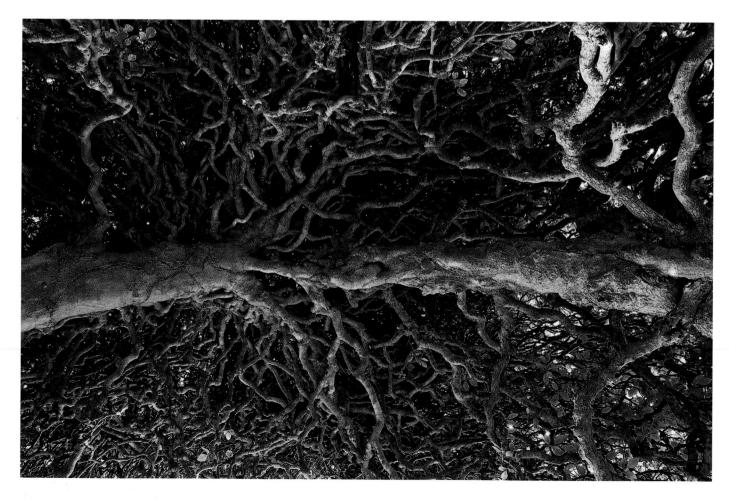

is dazzling in evening light. The hedge is 5 metres/16 feet high and the trees in it are about three hundred years old. It can take two gardeners a couple of months to shape its perfect contours. Four paths pierce the hedge, revealing a tracery of twigs inside it that is as impressive as the fan vaulting of a cathedral. Birds scoot down the beech-lined allées beyond at waist height. In spring the ground is carpeted with wild garlic; its smell lingers on deep into the summer.

Beyond the Circle is the Fountain Garden, built in 1994 to mark the tercentenary of the garden's creation. Chris Crowder looked at Robert Skyring's eighteenth-century map for a ground plan of this area and found, once again, that a circle and four cross axes were the basis of the original layout. A fountain now fills the circular space at the centre of the new design, and the axes are made from tunnels of red-twigged lime (*Tilia platyphyllos*). Chris has trained the trees into a regular lattice of precisely controlled branches that completely covers the sides and roofs of the tunnels in a *pièce de résistance* of perfect pruning. The sound of the fountain cannot drown the constant drone of the busy A6 that runs alongside the garden, but it manages to muffle and distract. From a bench in the Fountain Garden, the view is of green without seams. The lime tunnels are backed by the beech hedges, and the enormous trees in the Wilderness at the garden's far end are the final backdrop.

The architecture of Levens' impressive hedges, trees and allées is densely overlaid with flowers. There are only four full-time staff to manage the garden's 3.2 hectares/8 acres, and Chris Crowder takes a pragmatic and highly successful approach to the planting.

In the double Pastel Borders he repeats the same, small palette of plants again and again, making each border a reflection of the other. In mid-June, the borders are punctuated by regular explosions of *Crambe cordifolia* teamed with plants that include white *Geranium phaeum*, indigo delphiniums, white viola, the slug-resistant *Hosta sieboldiana*, day lilies, phlox and catmint. Clematis grows over sturdy wooden pyramids to bring another element of symmetry to the beds. Annuals and tender perennials are propagated in the garden's two greenhouses and used to prolong the colour until autumn. Chris calls his system 'gardening for maximum sensual impact and effect', and there can be no doubt that it works, both here and in the other impressive garden borders.

Head gardeners have always worked for an average of thirty years at Levens, and Chris is no exception. On an evening in midsummer, when oystercatchers wheel overhead and the scent of the roses swells with the fading light, it is easy to understand why.

Scampston

In late summer Scampston's Perennial Meadow is still blazing with colour and the grasses are coming into their own. Rich violet mounds of monarda nudge up against pale blue drifts of perovskia, blocks of marmalade-coloured heleniums, dusky pink echinacea, sages and sedums. Between them are great golden clumps of grasses such as *Panicum* 'Rehbraun', *Sesleria autumnalis* and *Deschampsia cespitosa*. Sit in one of the garden's low seats and you have a bee's-eye view through grasses and swathes of flowers to the dipping pool and fountain at its centre. The real bees are hard at work all over the garden, sparkling like striped jewels in the low evening light. Later in the year the flowers will die back, but then seed-heads will create a subtler but more enduring show throughout the winter.

The Perennial Meadow is at the heart of Scampston Hall's eighteenth-century Walled Garden. It is one element in a remarkable contemporary garden designed by Piet Oudolf for Sir Charles and Lady Legard. When Sir Charles inherited Scampston in 1994, the 1.8-hectare/4.5-acre walled garden was abandoned. For years it had been used only to grow Christmas trees and graze sheep; the Victorian glasshouses against its north wall were derelict. The Legards first met Piet Oudolf in 1998, while he was working with Arne Maynard on designs for the *Gardens Illustrated* garden at the Chelsea Flower Show. Their garden swept the board, simultaneously winning Best in Show and bringing New Naturalism to the heart of British horticulture. Oudolf was a pioneer of this novel style of planting, which takes nature as its model, creating a meadow-like arrangement of grasses and North American prairie plants such as rudbeckia, veronicastrum, eupatorium and monarda in merging, naturalistic drifts. The results of this approach appear effortless, but success depends upon an intimate knowledge of the needs and habits of each plant. Piet Oudolf and his wife, Anya, had run a successful nursery for years, and this gave Oudolf an expertise that allowed him to create planting plans in which the elements were finely balanced, with no plant so vigorous that it overwhelmed the others. Retaining this balance is one of the greatest challenges for Scampston's gardeners.

Scampston's naturalistic meadow is surrounded by the more formal elements of avenues, hedges and straight axes that divide the Walled Garden into eight separate rooms. The garden room is a very traditional feature in English gardens, but everything Piet Oudolf went on to do within this familiar structure was unexpected. The surprises start at the Plantsman's Walk, which is the garden entrance. This is a narrow path, flanked by a mixed border and the garden wall beyond it on one side, and a high beech hedge on the other. The path is in no hurry. It leads visitors around two sides of the garden before

LEFT Scampston's Perennial Meadow is a workhouse for insects. On a late summer evening the garden vibrates with the sounds of honey bees and bumblebees hard at work.
BELOW The vivid blue flowers of *Eryngium tripartitum* emerge from grasses growing in the Perennial Meadow.
BOTTOM Mounds and swathes of colour blend with the neutral tones of grasses in the Perennial Meadow.

49

permitting them to penetrate the high hedge. There is plenty to look at as they go, especially in spring, when the beds are packed with bulbs, peonies and the unusual and highly scented flowers of *Edgeworthia chrysantha*. Entry may be delayed, but it does not disappoint when the path eventually leads directly into a rectangular, hedge-lined space where waves of molinia grass (*M. caerulea* 'Poul Petersen') create an extraordinary, diagonal pattern across a perfectly smooth lawn.

Next door, the water in the square pool at the centre of the Silent Garden is still and black. A legion of clipped yew columns forms sombre lines on the lawn. Topiary is important at Scampston, and the Silent Garden is one of four topiary gardens within the Walled Garden. The Spring Box Garden and the Summer Box Garden are two narrow spaces to either side of the Perennial Meadow. They are both planted with cubes of box arranged in lines down their centres.

LEFT In autumn Scampston's beech hedges come into their own, blazing with colour until the depths of winter.
RIGHT In autumn the grove of katsuras (*Cercidiphyllum japonicum*) at the centre of the garden puts on a vibrant display of colour as the leaves turn shades of yellow, orange and red.

In the Spring Box Garden the cubes have convex tops, while those in the Summer Box Garden are concave. The Serpentine Garden consists of yew hedges that are gradually being clipped to form sinuous serpents with undulating tops.

The space next to the Serpentine Garden is dominated by an earth viewing mound that is surrounded by Yoshino cherries (*Prunus* x *yedoensis*) and wild flowers. From the top of the mound it is clear that Piet Oudolf's design for the Walled Garden is made up of a series of patterns, each one different, innovative and contemporary. And the show does not end with the summer. In autumn the grasses are at their finest, the beech hedges flare into colour, and the leaves of the katsuras (*Cercidiphyllum japonicum*) in the grove beside the Perennial Meadow begin to turn, filling the air around them with the sweet scent of burnt sugar.

Mount Stewart

In October, geese gather in noisy groups on the shores of Strangford Lough. Mount Stewart, a grey stone house surrounded by a broad terrace, faces south-west across the water and the distant Mountains of Mourne. The gardens around the house were designed and built by Edith, Countess of Londonderry. At this time of year the leaves on the richly planted trees around the lake have started to turn, but the parterre beds in the Italian Garden are still blazing with brightly coloured dahlias.

When Lady Londonderry's husband inherited Mount Stewart in 1915 she thought it a very dark and mournful place. Its only garden was a mile away and the house was surrounded by rough grass and holm oaks that jostled up to its windows. During the First World War Mount Stewart became a convalescent home. The family did not return to it until 1921. By this time local landlords were being asked to employ as many ex-soldiers as they could. Lady Londonderry grasped this opportunity and soon twenty ex-servicemen were helping her 'to make the grounds surrounding the house not only more cheerful and liveable, but beautiful as well'. They started work by levelling the land around the house, and Lady Londonderry began to order plant catalogues and draw up a design.

ABOVE Lady Londonderry planted a rich array of trees around Mount Stewart's nineteenth-century lake, and in autumn the water is stained with their bright colours.
RIGHT Two of the four dodos that give the Dodo Terrace its name. The ark – a reference to the Ark Club that Lady Londonderry founded in London – is seen against the backdrop of the Italian garden and the south façade of the house.

LEFT, ABOVE A view across the pool at the heart of the Spanish Garden, where pots of citrus stand at the water's edge. The steps link the Spanish Garden to the Italian Garden.
LEFT, BELOW The tall hedges of *Cupressocyparis leylandii* in the Spanish Garden were inspired by the arched hedges of Villa Gamberaia near Florence.

The garden that she created is an extraordinary combination of exotic plants, native and ornamental trees, bizarre and entirely unexpected statues, woodland and topiary extending across 39 hectares/97 acres. Its position on the Ards Peninsula gives the garden a very particular microclimate. The Irish Sea, which has the Gulf Stream running through it, is on the peninsula's east side and on its west is Strangford Lough. The garden faces south and it is entirely sheltered by woods. This unique combination of conditions creates a climate so mild and humid that it is almost sub-tropical. Lady Londonderry took full advantage of the site by packing the garden with unusual and tender plants from all over the world. She sponsored Frank Kingdon-Ward's plant hunting expeditions to China and was given many plants by him for the garden. She kept copious notes, recording the date of each new arrival and the weather conditions. She also recorded the exact planting position. If a plant had to be moved, she always made sure that its new planting place had the same aspect.

The first garden to be created was the Italian Garden on the south side of the house. It runs the entire length of the building and is surrounded by walls that she covered with camellias, *Ceanothus arboreus*, crinodendron and *Wisteria venusta*. She made Italianate parterres to east and west, planting a broad ribbon of grass to divide them. She packed the beds with a mixture of shrubs and flowering plants that would provide vivid colour from June until late autumn.

Mount Stewart is a museum for the strange and amusing statues designed by Lady Londonderry. She said that her inspiration for the herms on the balustrade of the Italian Garden came from the Villa Farnese at Caprarola in Italy. However, these herms are very much more eccentric than their Italian ancestors, for they support a strange troupe of bearded monkeys on their shoulders. The steps that link the Italian Garden to the house are flanked by clipped bay trees in pots that Lady Londonderry bought in Ghent in 1953. They are almost two hundred years old, and are said to be the largest pot-grown bays in Europe.

A flight of curved steps descends from the Italian to the Spanish Garden, which takes its name from a small pavilion roofed with green-glazed Spanish tiles. Lady Londonderry took her design for the layout from the floor of the Temple of the Winds, a folly on the garden's edge. A circular pool marks the garden's centre and stone channels divide the lawn that surrounds it. In summer, pots of lemons stand on the water's edge. The towering Leyland cypress arches that enclose the Spanish Garden are copied from the famous arched hedge of Villa Gamberaia in Florence.

Lady Londonderry's imagination ran wild on the Dodo Terrace, where an ark made from cement and an extraordinary tribe of animals, living and extinct, inhabit the garden's edge. The ark, the bashful dinosaur that peers out from the bushes, the vast and pig-like hedgehog, the fox, monkey, mermaid, frog and the four dodos all relate to Lady Londonderry's Ark Club. She founded the Ark in 1915 as a salon in wartime London. Its members were all her friends and each had to take the name of a real or mythical animal. Champagne flowed and painters, writers, politicians, soldiers and beautiful women played frivolous games together. After the war the Ark's meetings became more formal. Ramsay MacDonald, Stanley Baldwin and Neville Chamberlain all became members.

Other, less formal gardens surround the house. Among them are the Sunk Garden with its clematis-draped pergola, the Shamrock Garden where a topiary yew is cut into the shape of an Irish harp. The startling bed of begonias at the centre of the Shamrock Garden represents the Red Hand of Ulster. Lady Londonderry commissioned local craftsmen to make all of the stonework in the garden and to create her strange menagerie of animals. The balustrades, parapets, herms and pots were designed by her.

Wildlife, real and imaginary, is never lacking at Mount Stewart. In autumn, ducks swim through deep pools of colour reflected by the acers and katsura trees growing on the banks of the 2-hectare/5-acre lake excavated by the 3rd Marquess of Londonderry in 1840. Red squirrels scuttle between the trees. The lake is overlooked by the tower of Tir Nan Og (the Land of the Ever Young in Celtic mythology). This enclosed and private garden is the family burial ground, where the graves are overlooked by statues of Irish saints.

FAR LEFT *Clematis* 'Bill McKenzie' tumbles from the pergola surrounding the Sunk Garden.
CENTRE LEFT, ABOVE Yew topiary forms an Irish harp at the centre of the Shamrock Garden.
CENTRE LEFT, BELOW An archer takes aim, one of a number of topiary figures of humans, animals, birds and boats in the Shamrock Garden that were copied from the illuminations in a fourteenth-century psalter.
NEAR LEFT The tower behind Tir Nan Og, the family burial ground, seen from the far side of the lake. Japanese maples create a swathe of colour below it.

On a clear day the view from Bodnant in North Wales extends right across the tidal reaches of the meandering River Conwy to the peaks of Snowdonia. The house that enjoys this magnificent outlook was built in 1792. It is surrounded by an unmissable garden, a place of exceptional botanical interest that encapsulates the very best in early twentieth-century planting and design.

The transformation of Bodnant began in 1874 when Henry Pochin, an entrepreneurial chemist, industrialist and radical MP from Manchester, bought the Bodnant estate for his retirement. He transformed the simple Georgian building into the house that stands on the site today, built new cottages and planted trees on the estate. He commissioned Edward Milner to help him develop the garden, but many of the ideas were his own. He designed the gentle curve of the laburnum tunnel that still blazes with flowers each May, and built the handsome conservatory next to the house. It was also his idea to stabilize the banks of the Hiraethlyn, a narrow, fast-flowing brook that rushes along the floor of the Dell below the house, and to plant a collection of rare conifers to either side of it.

Pochin had six children, but only one son and a daughter survived infancy. Having disinherited his son, Pochin left Bodnant to his daughter, Laura, a campaigner, like her mother, for women's rights. Laura married Charles McLaren, who was to become the first Baron Aberconway. She was an accomplished gardener, both at Bodnant and at Château de la Garoupe, her house near Antibes in the south of France. On her death Laura was described in an obituary in *The Times* as one of the leading horticulturists in Europe. She passed her enthusiasm on to her son, Henry McLaren, and as soon as he graduated from Oxford in 1901 she entrusted the garden to his care.

Henry McLaren (1879–1953), who became the second Baron Aberconway, was a great plantsman and a gifted designer. In his hands Bodnant took on the shape it has today. Over a period of fifty years he enlarged the garden and developed two very different areas in it. The first centres on five hefty terraces that he cut from the west-facing slope below the house, designing them to fit cleverly around trees and other existing features in the garden. The second area was the steep-sided Dell far below the house, where he created a magnificent, naturalistic garden among the conifers planted by his grandfather. Lord Aberconway was particularly smitten by rhododendrons, and in 1908 he grew rhododendrons from seed collected in China by the great plant hunter E.H. Wilson. He worked closely with Frederick Puddle, his head gardener, and together they were pioneers in the production of rhododendron hybrids, many of which were awarded prizes by the Royal Horticultural Society and

OPPOSITE In spring, rhododendrons create waterfalls of colour down the steep sides of Bodnant's Dell.
BELOW The simple Georgian house at Bodnant was transformed at the end of the nineteenth century. It looks across the River Conwy to Snowdonia.
PAGES 60–61
LEFT Magnificent conifers grow in the Dell, including Wellingtonias (*Sequoiadendron giganteum*) and Douglas fir (*Pseudotsuga menziesii*).
CENTRE The River Hiraethlyn flows along the Dell, its banks lined with azaleas, rhododendrons, ferns and hostas.
RIGHT Rhododendrons and azaleas thrive in the Dell. Many of them are hybrids raised at Bodnant.

have subsequently become well known all over the world. It comes as no surprise to hear that Lord Aberconway became president of the Royal Horticultural Society in 1931, a post he held until his death in 1953.

Lord Aberconway's terraces anchor the house in the dramatic landscape that surrounds it. Each terrace is entirely different, and for the first-time visitor the garden unfolds as a series of magnificent surprises. The retaining walls of the sunny terraces create a series of warm microclimates, and in Lord Aberconway's lifetime the terrace beds soon became an exhibition space for surprisingly tender plants and botanical curiosities. He took to sponsoring the expeditions of other great plant hunters such as Kingdon-Ward, Joseph Rock, George Forrest and Frank Ludlow, and many plants in the garden were originally grown from the seeds that they brought home.

BELOW, LEFT A spectacular grouping that includes *Acer palmatum* 'Atropurpureum' and the Chilean firebush (*Embothrium coccineum*).
BELOW, RIGHT Bodnant's most famous feature is the Laburnum Arch, an unmissable sight from late May to mid-June. it is created from *Laburnum* x *watereri* 'Vossii'.

The first of the five terraces is known as the Upper Rose Garden, because its paved surface is punctuated by several stone-lined rose beds. The stone soaks up the sun and radiates warmth, coaxing the roses trained against the retaining wall to burst into flower by mid-May. Each flower bed is tightly packed with roses of a single variety: pink *Rosa* 'The Mayflower', white *R.* 'Margaret Merrill' and orange *R.* 'Aberconway'. Tiny, self-seeded campanulas and pools of pale saxifrage undermine any attempt at real formality in this perfumed, sun-soaked garden room, with its dramatic mountain view.

Broad stone steps link the Upper Rose Garden to the Croquet Terrace, with its long and perfectly smooth lawn. The stems of white *Wisteria floribunda* grip the stonework, its huge flowers filling the air with another layer of scent. At the base of the steps there is another enchanting wisteria, *W. venusta*, its downy, viridian leaves

and long white racemes trailing in the water of a deep pool. The beds beneath the curved retaining wall of the upper terrace are packed with shrubs. Pieris grows to the height of the wall, its new leaves adding a pink-ochre tint to beds that are already glowing with the flowers of tree peonies and of magnificent *Viburnum plicatum* and *V. macrocephalum* in spring.

Two broad staircases lead down to the Lily Terrace, where pink, white, red and yellow water lilies cover the surface of a long pool from midsummer until autumn sets in. The sheltered beds below the retaining wall are home to *Magnolia stellata* and *M. delavayi*, and a *M. grandiflora* x *virginiana* that has been trained to grow flat against the wall, as has the tender *Rhododendron fragrantissimum*, with its beautiful clusters of funnel-shaped white flowers, and sweetly scented *Eucryphia lucida* and *E. cordifolia*. In August, hydrangeas fill the beds with a profusion of blue and pink flowers.

The retaining wall beside the steps down to the pergola and the Lower Rose Terrace is studded with the golden flowers of *Rosa* 'Gardenia', which fills the warm air with its rich perfume. At its upper level, the two-tiered wooden pergola is lined with 'White Triumphator' tulips in spring. The fleshy, cerise, lanterns of *Crinodendron hookerianum* swathe the wall behind it, and informal clumps of the New Zealand satin flower (*Libertia grandiflora*) colonize the lower pergola.

A rectangular sheet of water lends its name to the Canal Terrace. At its southern end the view is stopped by the Pin Mill, a pale, stuccoed building that was salvaged and rebuilt in the garden by Henry, Lord Aberconway. Pin Mill marks the division between the two parts of the garden, the portal to an atmosphere so absolutely different that it seems to belong to another world. The narrow path that ducks down behind the mill leads to the Dell. Suddenly the air is laden with damp, mossy smells and the sound of running water. Progress is complicated by a choice of steep narrow paths, all of them leading towards the glittering silver ribbon of the Hiraethlyn. Bodnant is world famous for the beauty of the Dell in late spring, when rhododendrons, azaleas and magnolias transform its steep sides into a vertical palette splashed with astonishingly vivid swathes of colour.

RIGHT The sides of the Dell are so steep that they offer what is almost an aerial view of the narrow valley below.
OPPOSITE, ABOVE The Pin Mill stands on the Canal Terrace. It was originally built in Gloucestershire as a garden house in about 1730. Later it was used as a mill for making pins, and later still as a tannery. The second Lord Aberconway bought it and re-erected it here in 1939.
OPPOSITE, BELOW A branch of *Magnolia* x *soulangeana* 'Amabilis' flowers among the blossom of a white Japanese flowering crab apple.

BELOW The red sandstone walls and brick terraces of Powis Castle glow in the early morning sun.
OPPOSITE, ABOVE Japanese maples and amelanchiers cover the Apple Slope at the foot of the terraces.
OPPOSITE, BELOW Pots decorate the steps that link the garden's three terraces.

Powis Castle

Powis Castle is a distinctive building amply endowed with towers, turrets and battlements. Its magnificent garden falls away in a series of dramatic terraces made from the same red sandstone as the castle. Very few gardens were built in Britain in this Italianate, baroque style, and Powis is a lone survivor. It is one of the most important historic gardens in Wales, and also one of the National Trust's most adventurous and richly planted flower gardens.

During the Middle Ages the Welsh border was heavily fought over and an elevated position and long views made this the ideal site for a castle. By the sixteenth century, however, an enduring peace had come to the Borders. Powis was bought by the Herbert family, and like many other castles and fortresses, it was converted into a country house. At the end of the seventeenth century three terraces, each 152 metres/500 feet long, were blasted from the rugged slope below the castle. Archival evidence is scant, but it is thought that the design can be attributed to William Winde, architect of the garden terrace at Cliveden in Buckinghamshire.

At the beginning of the eighteenth century Adrian Duval, a Frenchman, designed a Dutch water garden on level ground below the terraces, but it was to be dismantled within a hundred years. The late 1770s saw William Emes called in to work his magic on the park. Emes was a devotee of 'Capability' Brown's naturalistic style, and it is said that he advised the Earl of Powis to level the garden terraces into a grassy slope. The Earl rejected this suggestion, but allowed Emes to transform the ridge opposite the castle into a beautiful wilderness composed of decorative trees and narrow, winding paths.

By the end of the century the terraces were under threat again, this time from neglect. Steps and balustrades began to give way and horses were reported grazing the parterres. The rigorous pruning regime applied to the yew hedges and obelisks planted on the terraces was relaxed. For a while they grew freely, but the nineteenth century saw an attempt to control their growth more tightly once again. Peter Hall, head gardener, describes the management of the Powis yews as a series of 'happy mistakes', which transformed their tight, geometric forms into the wonderfully generous, overblown and amorphous shapes that dominate the garden today.

The next important moment for Powis came at the beginning of the twentieth century when Violet, Countess of Powis and wife to the 4th Earl, took over the management of the garden. It was her ambition to propel Powis out of mediocrity and make the garden into 'one of the most beautiful, if not the most beautiful, in England and Wales'. Mission accomplished. Powis can most certainly lay claim to the title to which the Countess aspired, and it could probably carry off

The gigantic yew hedges that mark the eastern end of the terraces are the result of a series of happy accidents. They act as a pleasing foil to the precisely clipped trees in Lady Violet's formal Fountain Garden, below.

an additional award as one of Britain's most theatrical gardens. The site is dramatic, and so is the looming presence of the castle, but the real drama is played out between the formality of the terraces and the undisciplined yew trees and hedges that threaten to collapse, like dough left too long to rise, over the edges of the terraces.

Each of Powis's three terraces has a theme. The high walls of the top terrace shelter a magnificent display of 'tropical effect' planting made up of tender perennials. Most of the plants that the gardeners pack into the beds in early summer will have been overwintered or propagated in the glasshouses. By July the plants in the warm, south-facing beds have bulked up, and the intense blue flowers of *Salvia guaranitica* 'Indigo Spires' rub shoulders with ochre and yellow abutilons, pink fuchsias, the bronze leaves of *Musa coccinea* and the red flowers of *Cestrum elegans*. At the end of the season the beds are stripped down and many of the larger plants are discarded.

Lead shepherds and shepherdesses made by John van Nost in the seventeenth century do a perpetual dance across the balustrade of the second terrace, which takes its name from the aviary built against its retaining wall. The eastern end of the building is draped in a cascade of *Wisteria floribunda* and yellow *Rosa banksiae* 'Lutea'. Instead of birds the aviary shelters a *Ficus pumila* that papers the ceiling with its tiny leaves and wonderfully decorative chain ferns (*Woodwardia radicans*). Outside, a narrow, sun-baked bed is dedicated to plants from the Mediterranean, California and the southern hemisphere. It is heaven for cistus of every variety, broom, lavender and *Artemisia arborescens*, and for irises, whose gnarled rhizomes bask in the heat. Powis's top terrace is slightly tropical,

its second slightly Mediterranean, but the deep, heavy soil of the Orangery Terrace offers a perfect medium for entirely British double herbaceous borders. *Clematis* 'Jackmanii Superba' scrambles over metal hoops, as it has ever since the nineteenth century, and in early summer peonies, poppies and irises steal the show. The Orangery still shelters a few citrus trees each winter, and in summer they stand on the terrace outside. Beyond them the terrace disappears into the belly of the great yew hedge that tumbles down the hill at its far end. The path beyond it is a narrow channel between towering walls of venerable box.

In 1912, shortly after Violet, Countess of Powis, took over the garden, a storm felled several large elms. Their absence exposed a view over the kitchen garden and greenhouses that Violet considered 'detestable'. Her solution was to transform the kitchen garden by interplanting the fruit trees with a mixture of flowers that might be found in any Edwardian cottage garden. In the Fountain Garden beyond, the Countess's style became more formal. Clipped box lines an ample lawn with a fountain at its centre.

William Emes's Wilderness occupies a ridge overlooking the vast, velvety expanse of the Great Lawn. It is a romantic place, equally suited to lovers' trysts and solitary wandering. Emes's original planting was greatly enriched in the nineteenth century, when sessile oaks, Japanese cedars, tulip trees, Wellingtonias and many other interesting specimens were introduced. The stony ridge has an unexpected attribute: it has acid soil. This creates ideal conditions for the rhododendrons and azaleas that line the twisting paths. In spring the air is heavy with the sweet scent of the lovely, deciduous *Rhododendron luteum*.

RIGHT, ABOVE Buff-coloured
'Gloire de Dijon' roses flank the entrance
to the Orangery, where citrus trees
are overwintered.
RIGHT, BELOW The Orangery Terrace,
where plants flourish in the moist, deep
soil of two pairs of herbaceous borders.

Stourhead

Horace Walpole, an arbiter of eighteenth-century taste, described Stourhead as 'one of the most picturesque scenes in the world'. By this he meant that the serene beauty of the lake and the buildings surrounding it reminded him of the sort of semi-imaginary scenes that Claude had painted a century earlier in the Roman Campagna. But Stourhead was real. It was a living painting, created by a gifted amateur in the valley below his house. Henry Hoare II was untrained, but his natural talents combined with the architectural skills of Henry Flitcroft to produce a supreme example of the English landscape garden, a style that pushed Britain to the cutting edge of European garden design.

Henry Hoare II inherited Stourhead in 1741. The house had been designed for his father by Colen Campbell in a Palladian style, and built barely twenty years before. Hoare focused his attention on the area below the house, where the River Stour flowed through a deep valley. He began by having the river dammed to create a great mass of water. Then he laid out a path to lead down the steep side of the valley and around the lake. Henry Flitcroft, Hoare's favourite architect, was an associate of William Kent, the pioneer of the English landscape style. Hoare commissioned Flitcroft to design the classical and Gothic buildings that are the focal points of views across the water. The planting that surrounds the lake has been enriched by successive generations of the family. Hoare's grandson, Richard Colt Hoare, introduced many new and ornamental species of trees and shrubs, including *Rhododendron*

BELOW A view across the lake from the Temple of Apollo. The obelisk, which was first erected by Henry Hoare II in 1746, is just visible above the treetops. It had to be restored in 1853 after it was struck by lightning.

RIGHT The first view of the garden as seen from the Shades, the woods above the south side of the lake. In the distance the Temple of Apollo, built by Henry Flitcroft in 1765, catches the afternoon sun.

PAGES 74–75
LEFT A grebe floats peacefully in front of the magnificent tulip tree (*Liriodendron tulipifera*) that stands on the island in the centre of the lake.
RIGHT The path around the lake allows visitors occasional carefully composed glimpses of the pleasures to come. Here the Pantheon comes briefly into view.

ponticum, eight varieties of maple and twelve of oak. In the mid-nineteenth century about twenty new conifer species were added to the collection, including forest giants like the western red cedar (*Thuja plicata*). Enormous numbers of new azaleas and hybrid rhododendrons were planted in the twentieth century until, in 1946, the house was given to the National Trust.

Hoare made no visual connection between the house and the valley below. But this is no reason to ignore the house. Only by making your way across to the mellow, sandstone building and starting your walk from its south façade can you truly appreciate the impact of his magnificent garden. A level lawn leads away from the house, past Edwardian shrubberies of azaleas and rhododendrons. In August, hydrangeas make great cushions of flowers and low-flying swallows quarter the lawn. A path at the lawn's far end leads into dense woods on the side of the valley. Almost at once the first of Hoare's carefully devised views opens out. It is of a beautiful classical building framed by trees on the opposite side of the valley. The building at the centre of this view, the first in a series of living paintings, is the Temple of Apollo. Flitcroft designed several temples at Stourhead and Hoare's educated friends would have recognized the buildings at the centre of the scenes unfolding before them as a series of visual quotations from Virgil's *Aeneid*. Hoare was steeped in classical culture after three years' travel in Europe, much of it in Italy, and his new garden gave him a personal foothold in antiquity.

A few more steps take you among the soaring silvered trunks of the beech trees that dominate the planting on this side of the valley. Enormous rhododendrons line the path. In August the huge white flowers of *R*. 'Polar Bear' fill the air with their sweet scent. The next turn in the path reveals a view of the Pantheon, perfectly framed by trees. The view snaps shut as suddenly and completely as it unfolded, leaving you once again surrounded by trees. A child's laughter rings out, but this huge landscape absorbs 350,000 visitors a year and even on this busy day the paths are empty, the child invisible.

By the time you reach the bottom of the hill you will know that you are following a hesitant route, a path much given to meander and delay. Hoare designed the circuit around the lake to be followed in an anti-clockwise direction. Don't hurry, for this is a circular walk and you have no particular destination. Take time to notice the trees and the meticulously framed views across the water. At the lake's far end you get your first glimpse of a landscape beyond the self-contained world of the garden. This is the magnificent valley of Six Wells Bottom, where the River Stour has its source. On the lake's far side the path dips down towards the water, where a tiny peninsula is planted with a miniature grove of silver birch that serves to distract you from an abrupt change

LEFT, ABOVE A tulip tree close to the house is surrounded by bluebells in spring
LEFT, BELOW A white rhododendron sheds its blossom on to the garden bench below.
RIGHT A nymph (copied from an original in the Vatican Gardens) sleeps in the Grotto. The inscription, by Alexander Pope, reads:

Nymph of the Grot, these sacred springs I keep
And to the Murmur of these Waters sleep:
Ah! Spare my slumbers, gently tread the cave
And drink in silence or in silence lave.

FAR RIGHT At the entrance to the Grotto, a statue in painted lead of a river god points the way towards the Pantheon.
PAGES 78–79 At dawn, a nesting swan is undisturbed on an island in front of the Pantheon, which was built by Henry Flitcroft in 1753.

in your surroundings. Suddenly the path is densely shaded. A pitted limestone arch rears up ahead, and ferns grow to either side. This is the Grotto, home to the water nymphs, the inscription over the entrance declares. And here is Virgil's nymph, asleep by a sacred pool in the circular room at the heart of the Grotto. Her pale body illuminates the shadows, and spring water rushing into the pool cools the air. During the particularly hot summer of 1762, Henry Hoare began to use the nymph's bath as his plunge pool, an experience so delicious that he described

it as 'Asiatick luxury'. A window cut from the limestone wall opposite the bath makes a rough-edged frame for a perfectly composed view of the village church and the bridge.

Flitcroft's buildings have a symbolic purpose, linking Stourhead to classical myths and pastoral poetry, but they double as the destinations that the walk would otherwise lack, spurring visitors on today, just as they have always done. The next entertainment on route is the Gothic Cottage. Henry Hoare is known to have visited Walpole's Gothick

LEFT, ABOVE The Gothic Cottage, remodelled in 1806 for Henry Colt Hoare, to give it a more 'Gothick' appearance.
LEFT, BELOW The Temple of Flora was the first of Henry Hoare's garden buildings. It stands above a natural spring known as Paradise Well.
RIGHT The Temple of Apollo, seen in the eerie light of an approaching storm.

house in Strawberry Hill, and the cottage is thought to be a tribute to what he found there. It stands in the shade of a majestic fern-leaved beech (*Fagus sylvatica* var. *heterophylla* 'Aspleniifolia') planted by the 6th Baronet in the first half of the twentieth century. When its leaves turn in autumn, the cosy domesticity of the scene is swept away by high drama. Stourhead is intensely dramatic at this time of year, for the lake reflects the trees, doubling the extent of autumn colour.

Leave the cottage and the Pantheon is suddenly upon you, startlingly large and close. It is here, for the first time, that we are granted a full view across the lake towards the Temple of Flora on the opposite shore. Flitcroft took inspiration for the Pantheon from its original in Rome, and Stourhead's temple to the gods is the largest and most important building in the garden. Hoare had a stove installed so that he could picnic at the Pantheon on cool days. His guests ate in the shadow of Michael Rysbrack's imposing statue of Hercules, Diana, goddess of their host's favourite pastime, and Flora, goddess of gardens.

Hoare's circuit of the lake reaches a climax at the Temple of Apollo, high up among the trees on the hillside. The circular building is dedicated to the sun god, and his face blazes from the centre of the ceiling, surrounded by a halo of golden rays. The view from this elevated point stretches right across the lake and encompasses the wooded hills to either side of it.

As you descend the hill from Apollo's temple and make your way back towards the village, you will feel that you have reached the end of a journey. It has been an intense experience, for Henry Hoare's hand has never left your shoulder; he has manipulated your moods and defined your experience, leading and enticing you through a series of different atmospheres and sensations, and never leaving you for one moment to your own devices. If you have played along, going around the lake in the anti-clockwise direction that he favoured and pausing to consider and absorb every view that he prepared for you, you will leave Stourhead elated, and deeply satisfied.

Hidcote

The history of the garden at Hidcote Manor begins in 1907, when a wealthy American widow called Gertrude Winthrop decided to buy the entire hamlet of Hidcote Bartram near Chipping Campden, with its ten cottages, seventeenth-century manor house and 121 hectares/300 acres of land. At the beginning of the twentieth century Chipping Campden was at the centre of the Arts and Crafts movement, and of a lively and creative community of painters, gardeners, architects, sculptors, jewellers, glass makers and craftsmen of all kinds. Burne-Jones, Sargent and Elgar were often guests at local parties, and many Americans had chosen to settle in the area. Mrs Winthrop was accompanied by her son, Lawrence Johnston. She may have been a socialite, but he was altogether a quieter type. Johnston was thirty-six by the time he moved to Hidcote. He had spent much of his childhood in France, travelled in Italy, taken a history degree at Trinity College, Cambridge, and experimented with farming in Northumberland. The garden was to become the focus and purpose of his life. He had a good idea of its importance by the time he died, but even he cannot have suspected that it would become the most influential garden of the twentieth century, spawning generation after generation of gardens divided into 'rooms' in a style that was originally somewhat Italianate, but came to be seen as so intrinsically British that its true origins are all but forgotten.

When Johnston arrived at Hidcote he had no formal training in horticulture or botany, but he was already borrowing books about garden design from the Royal Horticultural Society's Lindley Library. The land surrounding Hidcote was not a particularly promising site for a garden. It was an exposed and windswept slope, and the only trees growing anywhere near the house were a cedar of Lebanon and a ragged clump of beeches. Undaunted and blissfully ignorant, Johnston spend half a dozen years levelling the sloping site, laying paths and creating long vistas. He also planted the hedges that would divide the garden into rooms. The multicoloured tapestry hedges of intermingling holly and green and copper beech are one of the garden's great features. Johnston worked with enormous energy and by the time the First World War broke out he had made the axis that runs east–west from the old cedar tree, and the Maple Garden, White Garden and Old Garden were all well established.

In midsummer, the Old Garden is a sensory overload of heavily perfumed flowers in pastel shades. Staddle stones line the path, soft blue, pink or white flowers overflow from the beds, and roses and mock orange compete to saturate the air with their scents. This cottage-garden style of planting was typical of Arts and Crafts gardeners in the area, but Johnston was rapidly becoming a more discerning plantsman than most of his contemporaries. He left Hidcote in 1914 to fight with the Northumberland Hussars, abandoning the garden to the care of a skeleton team of gardeners. He was injured twice during the war, gassed once and left for dead. Nevertheless, he returned home after four years and designed the Stilt Garden and the Pillar Garden as soon as he had recovered from his injuries. In the Stilt Garden Johnston seemed to take inspiration from France rather than Italy. Hornbeams, their long thin legs exposed by pruning, flank the end of the east–west axis, leading the eye towards wrought-iron gates known affectionately as 'the gates of heaven', because the gently sloping ground makes them seem to enclose nothing but sky.

The post-war years were Hidcote's glory days. The garden now covered 4 hectares/10 acres and Johnston had begun to subscribe to plant-hunting expeditions. After his mother's death in 1926 he even accompanied Cherry Ingram to South Africa, and George Forrest to China. It is no coincidence that a number of plant species have 'Hidcote' among their varieties. At home, the planting in the garden grew richer and richer, each border minutely planned for both colour and succession. Norah Lindsay, a garden designer with a house at Sutton Courteney, was a great friend to Johnston in this period, and she is thought to have persuaded him to plant the Rose Walk at Hidcote. Johnston and Lindsay feared that shrub roses would be forgotten as more and more new, repeat-flowering roses appeared on the market. The Rose Walk is a celebration of the shrub roses bred in France during the eighteenth and nineteenth centuries. Gallica, Moss, Damask, Hybrid Perpetual, Alba and Centifolia roses create a single, magnificent display of colour at the end of June. However, bulbs, shrubs and herbaceous perennials prolong the display in the Rose Walk from late spring until autumn sets in.

By the end of the 1920s Johnston had begun to spend the winter at Serre de la Madone, his house near Menton in the south of France. Eventually he abandoned Britain altogether, and in 1948 the garden was handed over to the National Trust.

BELOW, LEFT The hornbeams in the Stilt Garden are pleached, leaving their trunks clean, like stilts. The Red Borders are just visible in the background.
BELOW, RIGHT A view towards the gates at the western end of the Stilt Garden.

LEFT A solitary gardener wheels a barrow through the magnificent trees of the Beech Alley.

Don't go to Hidcote in a hurry. Give it the chance to swallow you up, confuse you with detail and entertain you with the densely sewn tapestry of its planting. Take time to enjoy a sudden change of pace, or an unexpected view across the surrounding landscape. Lawrence Johnston did not take his lead from Lutyens or Jekyll, whose gardens were linked to the house by a powerful architectural logic. Instead, Hidcote seems to develop as a stream of consciousness, an ever-expanding suite of rooms with no perceivable structure. It incorporates Italianate rooms, French parterres, a woodland garden, a stream garden and the skilfully 'borrowed' landscapes of the eighteenth-century garden. These influences are foreign and far reaching, yet they are combined to create the archetypal English garden, a blueprint that continues to exert its influence to this day.

BELOW, LEFT The Hidcote year begins in spring, with dense displays of tulips in the Old Garden. BELOW, RIGHT Lawrence Johnston used to keep flamingos in this pool at the centre of the Pine Garden.

Great Dixter

Great Dixter was the home of Christopher Lloyd, one of the most unorthodox and influential figures of twentieth-century gardening. His books, articles and the garden itself have combined to inspire, delight, provoke and bemuse a generation of British gardeners. Lloyd lived and gardened at Great Dixter until his death in 2006. For the last fifteen years of Lloyd's life, Fergus Garrett worked alongside him as head gardener. Dixter is now controlled by the Great Dixter Charitable Trust, and Fergus Garrett continues to manage it. He is committed to maintaining the garden as an innovative and dynamic centre for horticulture and plantsmanship.

Christopher Lloyd inherited Great Dixter from his parents. His father, Nathaniel Lloyd, had bought the derelict, timber-framed house, a few barns and a farm in 1909. He chose Edwin Lutyens as his architect, and in his hands the fifteenth-century house was beautifully restored and enlarged. The rough, nettle-infested area around it was transformed into a series of yew-lined garden rooms, broad terraces, orchards and courtyards. Barns and cowsheds were woven into the design and transformed into mellow garden buildings.

By the time Christopher Lloyd inherited Great Dixter in 1972, the garden was very well established. His mother, Daisy Lloyd, had been a knowledgeable plantswoman and a skilled gardener, and Christopher had worked alongside her from a very early age. In his hands, the garden soon became famous for the use of exotic plants, unorthodox colour combinations, meadow gardening and skilled planting that extends the season from March to the darkest depths of November.

Go to Dixter in early July and you will find the party in full swing. Canna, one of Lloyd's ancient dachshunds, barks a continuous warning from the front porch, but some of the guests are already the worse for wear. The flowers in the hedge-lined High Garden above the house have begun to spill over the paths, as if the plants themselves had decided to close the place to visitors. Everything is a little loucher and less disciplined than it might have been earlier in the year, and the atmosphere is relaxed and festive. Anything goes in this great, colourful celebration. Even the hedges are generous, their abundant bellies swelling out over the paths. The tile-hung roofline of the house can be glimpsed between towering explosions of *Verbascum* 'Christo's Yellow Lightning' that stride through the dense and complex planting. Cerise-pink pools of lychnis nudge up to crimson poppies, and battalions of 'Velvet Queen' sunflowers,

A view taken across the Long Border to the house in late spring, when bulbs dominate the garden. Constant maintenance and renewal will keep the border in flower until winter sets in.

pink fuchsias and waves of lemon-yellow day lilies. Swathes of *Calamagrostis* 'Karl Foerster', a purple-seeded grass, catch the breeze. These are the sort of surprising colour combinations for which Lloyd became famous. In his own words, he took it 'as a challenge to combine every sort of colour effectively'.

Great Dixter's most celebrated feature is probably the Long Border, which extends for 60 metres/200 feet on level ground below the sloping High Garden. It is legendary both for its size (it is also 4.5 metres/15 feet deep) and for its high-octane delivery of colour and interest throughout the year. The border represents fifty years' work by Daisy Lloyd, fifty by Christopher himself and another twenty by Fergus Garrett, who describes the Long Border as 'the place where . . . successional planting is practised to its fullest'. Successional planting is the secret of Great Dixter's long season. Christopher Lloyd developed a system for orchestrating the performance of bulbs and self-seeded plants, shrubs, perennials, climbers and enormous quantities of annuals, so that the show in the Long Border would go on and on. He underplanted and interplanted, ensuring that as one plant died down, another would always leap up to take its place. The show begins with snowdrops in the depths of winter. Thousands of tulips, which Fergus now plants in ever-increasing numbers, emerge through the spring foliage of April, and that's just the beginning. By July, the border is already being topped up with the annuals that are grown at Dixter in vast numbers. This style of gardening may look artless, but it is meticulously planned, and backstage the maintenance is continuous. Fergus makes changes to the planting each year, just as he and Christopher always did. Each year it becomes fuller and more vibrant.

The Barn Garden on the other side of the house is also in full swing. This garden and the Sunk Garden below it are enclosed on all sides by barns or hedges. In the original Lutyens design, this was a grass area that might have been used as a croquet lawn. During the First World War troops were lodged in the house, and the Barn Garden was put down to vegetables. By the end of the war it was in a terrible mess and Nathaniel Lloyd, who had been greatly inspired by working alongside Lutyens, decided to redesign it himself. The Brunswick fig that Lutyens planted against the barn wall still thrives, but the garden has developed continuously. When her husband died, Daisy Lloyd pulled out the yuccas that he had planted and replaced them with crab apples. Christopher never liked them, and after his mother's death he ripped them up and filled the space with the *Osmanthus delavayi* that grows there today, clipped into neat balls. The broad beds on the terrace are filled with cottage garden

BELOW, LEFT Christopher Lloyd was famous for his unorthodox use of colour, and Fergus Garrett's planting schemes continue to surprise and delight.
BELOW, CENTRE The deep purple swaying heads of the ornamental grass *Calamagrostis* 'Karl Foerster' bring colour and movement to the High Garden.
BELOW, RIGHT Most of the tulips in the garden are lifted, sun-baked, and then replanted in the autumn.

flowers. Christopher Lloyd could occasionally be found beside the pool in the Sunk Garden, bashing out an article with a laptop balanced on his knees.

Lutyens built a brick archway to link the Barn Garden to the Wall Garden next door. There used to be turf underfoot, but as visitor numbers grew, Lloyd knew that he must put down something more solid. He came up with the idea of a mosaic made from Dungeness shingle. It depicts his two dachshunds, Canna and Dahlia. The eyes and nose of each dog are made out of pebbles from Derek Jarman's garden at Prospect Cottage at Dungeness, Kent. The new hard surface allowed Lloyd to experiment with the pots that now provide an ever-changing backdrop to the Wall Garden. They contain a battery of non-hardy plants that need plenty of shade and water. In the Wall Garden all their needs are catered for, and as soon as a plant goes over, it is replaced by another from the nursery. Lloyd and Garrett developed a similar system with tiered ranks of pots outside the front door of the house.

A traditional rose garden was part of Lutyens' original plan. After many decades, the roses ceased to thrive and Christopher Lloyd provoked national outrage by grubbing them up and writing an article describing the sound of their roots being torn out of the ground as 'music to my ears'. He left the stone-lined beds in place, but the space was transformed into the Exotic Garden, and planted up with an experimental combination of tender and brightly coloured plants to create a tropical effect. This is the only part of the garden that has a single climax that lasts from August to September. It is not planted up until June, when the nights are warmer. Dahlias and cannas provide colour. They are combined with bamboos, begonias, morning glory, the Japanese banana (*Musa basjoo*), *Arundo donax* and colocasias. Everything grows at bionic speed, and by September the paths between the beds are barely visible.

Great Dixter's wildflower meadows were originally developed by Daisy Lloyd, who lured orchids into the garden's wild places and introduced camassias, polyanthus, snakeshead fritillaries, wild daffodils and crocuses into the dry moat, the rough grass in front of the house and the orchard. Nearly a century has passed, and the wildflower meadows become richer every year. They are carefully managed, and cut only in August, when all the flowers have shed their seeds. Nothing has ever stood still in this dynamic place, and Fergus Garrett is now extending the wildflower meadows into the fields below the garden. Whatever next? Who knows, but it's bound to be interesting.

Late summer in East Ruston's Desert Wash, a garden designed to resemble parts of Arizona where rain falls only once or twice a year, engraving deep channels in the ground.

East Ruston Old Vicarage

Head north-east from Norwich and you are soon in big-sky country. Someone swept the furniture from this landscape years ago, tearing out trees and hedges to make great blank spaces that stretch almost unhindered to the North Sea. When Alan Gray and Graham Robeson bought the Old Vicarage at East Ruston in 1973, the house was entirely exposed to relentless winds. They used Italian alders, Monterey pines and eucalyptus to make a first line of defence against the wind, and simultaneously enclose about 0.8 hectares/2 acres of rough grassland around the house. In August ripe corn bleaches the fields, and the Old Vicarage garden appears as a green cube afloat on a blond sea.

It is hard to believe that Robeson and Gray did not initially intend to make a garden. Their first impulse was just to restore some of the original field boundaries swept away by the grain barons of the 1960s, thus recreating valuable habitats for wildlife. Almost forty years later, the initial 2 acres have expanded to 32 acres/13 hectares, and the reinstated fields have been transformed into the tesserae in a brightly coloured mosaic of interlocking gardens, each with its own unique character. Gray and Robeson take their inspiration from a wide range of styles and periods, and their ever-expanding garden is a visual encyclopaedia of garden design. Holland, New Zealand, California and the Mediterranean are all represented. There are wildflower, woodland and vegetable gardens, avenues of apples, holm oaks, silver birch, acacia and hydrangea. There are sunken gardens and raised beds, gravel gardens and terraces.

Hemmed in on one side by the Monterey pines that form a windbreak, the path from the car park gives nothing away. It is not until you arrive on the drive beside the house that the performance begins. Here there is a curious roundabout where pink-faced dahlias mill about like pedestrians beneath robinias clipped to resemble road signs and bollards of variegated holly. A gate in the wall leads to a second enclosure where the glowing, bronze faces of *Aeonium arboreum* 'Zwartkop' emerge on craning necks among a lush, late-summer planting of oranges, yellows and golds. The gate to the outside world is surmounted by a grand coat of arms on a terracotta plaque. How endearing to hear that it belongs to neither Gray nor Robeson. It is the insignia of the City of Manchester, and they bought it purely for the motto inscribed beneath it: *Consilio et Labore* (by counsel and labour), a good maxim for gardeners. A gate in the wall leads to the North Garden, where the towering russet stems of *Tetrapanax papyriferus* overhang the path, and the atmosphere changes abruptly once again, from light to dark, from vibrant colour to every shade of green. This enfilade of densely planted rooms is

little more than an *antipasto*, a series of *amuses bouches*, for the main course is yet to come.

Robeson and Gray's first set piece is the Dutch Garden opposite the house. Here the perfectly clipped, box-lined beds are overflowing with purple verbenas, orange dahlias and grasses. Spheres of golden holly (*Ilex aquifolium* 'Golden King') join forces with dusky box pyramids and globes to contain the riot at ground level and create the hint of formality that offsets the extraordinarily generous planting. This formality becomes more pronounced in the King's Walk, which makes the main vista from the house. Here yew obelisks lead the eye between gradually receding beech hedges to a pavilion that eventually stops the view.

This is a garden of rapid gear changes, and it is no surprise to find yourself propelled from the cool, green grandeur of the King's Walk to the intense heat of the Red and Purple Border. In this long narrow space, topiary watering cans flank the path and cerise dahlias jostle against soft pink alstroemerias and astilbes, puce snapdragons and purple verbenas. Gray and Robeson are a pair of pyrotechnicians – their garden is a series of firework displays – but they perfectly understand the need to punctuate the design with quieter interludes. The beech hedges that line the Green Court enclose no more than two holm oak arches. It is a tranquil green box of light, a sorbet to refresh the palette before the next pyrotechnic display of colour.

Anyone living in an exposed place dreams of escape from the constant badgering of the wind. Most plant windbreaks, but few would think of excavating the enormous space that is East Ruston's Sunk Garden. A sunken garden might give away all its secrets at once to anyone looking from above. This potential problem has been avoided by the blocks of yew that surround Bill Cordaroy's glass and steel fountain at the garden's centre. They obstruct the view across the densely furnished space, making it imperative to enter the garden and explore. Roses are a common theme in the raised beds, but their bedfellows – *Agave ferox*, for example – are often unexpected.

Nothing in the Sunk Garden proves quite engaging enough to distract from an intriguing wooden structure on its west side. Robeson and Gray refer to it as a pergola, but as you push your way through the vines that smother the entrance, the idea of a pergola is replaced by that of a long house in some distant jungle. Whatever its inspiration, this is a truly modern garden building. The low doorway gives no hint of the enormous scale of the space beyond. The wooden building is open sided, but bamboos rush in to make an exotic green wall to either side of the nave-like room. The balcony at its far end looks out over the Exotic Garden. Here Robeson and Gray have written their own entry in the encyclopaedia of garden design, a space so unusual and intrinsically modern that it has no precedent. Two raised pools dominate the centre of the oblong space, their broad rims clad in lead. Water lilies and papyrus grow in one, and in the other is an intriguing and truly contemporary fountain by Giles Raynor, one of Britain's leading water sculptors. Planting in the beds to either side takes its tone from the vine-clad, jungle long house at the garden's far end. The beds are packed with Japanese bananas (*Musa basjoo*), tetrapanax and the vast leaves of paulownias that are cut back to a stump each year. Red orach, canna lilies and fiery dahlias bring a final burst of heat to late summer.

Beyond the Exotic Garden the story continues to unfold in woods and meadows, vegetable plots and orchards, and in the extraordinary Desert Wash, a landscape inspired by the Arizona desert. Here 500 tonnes of flint were imported to create a landscape in turmoil. The planting is designed to look as though opportunists have germinated at will, taking advantage of a rare rainstorm that has flooded the area, gouging out channels among the stones. Puyas thrive here, sending up their great flower spikes in early summer. California poppies create great sheets of colour among agaves, dasylirion and yuccas.

RIGHT, ABOVE Clipped holm oak arches frame an urn in the Green Court, a calm, beech-lined room..

RIGHT, BELOW The Exotic Garden, where Giles Raynor's unusual fountain sprays water in on itself to create a shape that resembles a whirlwind.

PAGES 98–99

LEFT, ABOVE The gaily striped Happisburgh lighthouse seen from the Winter Garden. The path is bordered with evergreen oak (*Quercus ilex*) and Chusan palms (*Trachycarpus fortunei*).

LEFT, BELOW The topiary in the Red and Purple Border is cut into the shape of gigantic watering cans.

CENTRE, ABOVE Plants flourish in the hot, dry beds of the south-facing terraces in the Mediterranean Garden. Each terrace is backed by a retaining wall that acts like a giant storage heater, soaking up the sun's warmth all day and releasing it at night.

CENTRE, BELOW The cornfield is planted with a rich and colourful mixture of old cornfield weeds. The mix is varied each year.

RIGHT, ABOVE The Apple Walk frames a view of Happisburgh church. The walk is lined with *Nepeta* 'Six Hills Giant' that is clipped repeatedly to ensure successive flowerings.

RIGHT, BELOW The pavilion at the heart of the Mediterranean Garden houses a series of interesting aerial photographs of the garden.

Beth Chatto Gardens

Moving house is always difficult. Some people complicate matters further by adding ideal gardening conditions to their list of priorities. Not the Chattos. By the time they built a house on the edge of their fruit farm in Suffolk, both Beth and her husband, Andrew, were experienced gardeners. Why did they choose to build between a boggy hollow and a stretch of sun-baked gravel so dry that even weeds could not survive? They were undaunted by these challenges because Andrew Chatto was already an expert in plant ecology. Both he and Beth knew that they could transform the superficial disadvantages of the site by selecting plants naturally suited to the conditions that it offered, an approach that was later defined by the catchphrase 'the right plant in the right place'. Beth also took courage from her long friendship with Sir Cedric Morris, renowned for his painting and his extraordinary knowledge of plants.

Over fifty years have passed since 1960, when Andrew, Beth and their two daughters moved into the new house. Since then Beth Chatto's fame as a plantswoman, garden designer and author has spread worldwide. She has won ten gold medals at the Chelsea Flower Show and received the Royal Horticultural Society's Victoria Medal of Honour. This remarkable career has been built upon the blighted land that once surrounded her home, land that she transformed into one of the most famous gardens in Britain.

When the Chattos first moved to the new house, cows grazing the hollow below it stood up to their hocks in mud. This boggy area was gradually transformed into the Water Gardens, where four large pools sit, each one slightly lower than the last. Water is always in gentle movement here, filling the air with its sound. Enormous swamp cypresses tower above the pools, their awkward, knobbly 'elbows' bursting out of the flowerbeds at their feet. The planting around the pools is a bold combination of swathes and clumps. By mid-August there is no sign of the marsh marigolds and candelabra primulas that lit up the water's edge in spring, but now the spear-shaped leaves of *Thalia dealbata* thrust out of the water, its curious, crêpe-paper flowers borne at head height. There are clumps of pink astilbe and stands of brilliant day lilies and rudbeckias, but Beth Chatto does not depend on colour for her effect. Magisterial clumps of gunnera jostle with miscanthus, bamboos and *Phormium tenax*. The real delight of this part of the garden comes from the clever contrasts that she has created between the shapes, colours and textures of leaves.

Shut your eyes in the Gravel Garden on a hot August morning and breathe in. The warm air is laden with the spicy Mediterranean scents of lavender and cistus, nepeta, sage, rosemary and any number of other grey-leaved plants. A rare overnight downpour

Planting in the shade of the enormous
swamp cypresses that grow beside the
pools of the Water Gardens.

has left the leaves of bergenias cradling tiny pools of water, and raindrops form dazzling beads on a spider's web. Two deep borders run along either side of the garden. Between them is a sea of gravel punctuated by a series of densely planted island beds. A gravel mulch laid over the beds protects the plants' roots in winter. It also serves to eliminate hard edges and confuse the boundaries between paths, beds and borders. By August the lush leaves and flowers of early summer have died down, and grey-leaved plants and grasses dominate the scene. Come at any time of year and there is something to see, for Beth Chatto is expert in creating the associations of texture, shape and colour that she describes as 'pictures'. When she began work on this part of the garden in 1991 it was an experiment. Global warming had not yet entered popular consciousness, but this patch of Essex has the lowest rainfall in Britain. Couple this with soil made up of 6 metres/20 feet of gravel laid over clay, and opportunities for the traditional gardener were reduced to almost zero. Beth Chatto drew on her husband's expert knowledge of plant habitats, and on observations of her own made during a trip to New Zealand, where she saw native plants thriving among the rocks on a dry riverbed. In the twenty years since it was first planted, the garden has never been irrigated. There have been moments of anguish, but over the years the planting has been fine tuned so that now the garden is made up only of plants perfectly adapted to its conditions. When she began her experiment, Beth Chatto thought that its results might be of interest in areas afflicted by a hosepipe ban, but in the climate-conscious twenty-first century, the garden is of interest to anyone, anywhere.

As summer nears its end, the colours in the Gravel Garden become ever subtler.

BELOW, LEFT The magnificent Palm House built in the 1840s by Richard Turner and Decimus Burton, takes its form from the upturned hull of a ship.
BELOW, RIGHT The interior of the Temperate House, the world's largest surviving Victorian glass building.

There are many good reasons for visiting Kew Gardens. You might go there to escape the noise and bustle of central London, for Kew is an enormous green lung, a vast and tranquil space on the banks of the Thames. However, the gardens have very much more to offer than peace and solitude. They are home to the biggest plant collection in the world, and the garden landscape is scattered with intriguing follies, glasshouses – both historic and modern – ancient trees and an enormous variety of separate and very distinctive gardens. All of these things are entertaining for the visitor, but Kew is underpinned by rigorous intellectual purpose. It is internationally renowned as a centre for botanical research and conservation, and the herbarium and library are used by thousands of visitors every year, and by students at Kew's School of Horticulture. All this would surely be enough, but Kew also occupies an important position in the history of British horticulture and landscape architecture.

Many familiar names are bound up in a story that unfolds from the early seventeenth century, when James I had a hunting lodge near the river to the south of Kew. This royal connection evolved in the eighteenth century, when each generation of the royal family contributed something to the ever-expanding garden. In 1728 Kew became a royal residence, and Queen Caroline commissioned Charles Bridgeman to redesign the gardens. In 1729 William Kent began to adorn the site with garden buildings. There was another spate of intense activity after the death of the Prince of Wales in 1751 when his widow, Princess Augusta, engaged William Chambers to design twenty-five decorative garden buildings. Many of them have disappeared over the years, but his pagoda survives to tower over the garden, creating one of the iconic images of Kew. Some of the trees planted for Princess Augusta also live on, including a venerable pagoda tree (*Styphnolobium japonicum*), its branches almost horizontal, and a maidenhair tree (*Ginkgo biloba*) planted in 1762, less than forty years after the first ginkgos were brought to Europe from China. By the time Princess Augusta died in 1772, there were already 3,400 plant species growing at Kew.

Kew continued to thrive and expand under the guidance of Joseph Banks, the distinguished plant hunter and botanist, who was particularly interested in promoting the study of plants of economic importance. Only after Banks' death in 1820 did the garden's fortunes decline. After a period of neglect, the Crown handed Kew over to Parliament, and William Hooker came from Glasgow Botanic Garden to run it. He was soon joined by his son, Joseph Hooker, a friend of Charles Darwin and himself an eminent botanist. Joseph ran the gardens for twenty years after his father died.

LEFT, ABOVE In spring sheets of chionodoxa cover the grass in front of Kew Palace, which was once the favourite home of George III, and his retreat during bouts of madness.
LEFT, BELOW A wind stirs the branches in the wood around Queen Charlotte's Cottage, where the royal family used to picnic. In May the ground is carpeted with bluebells.

RIGHT, ABOVE Two Japanese cherries, *Prunus* 'Horinji' and *Prunus lannesiana* 'Matsumae Hanazone', stand in front of the wild cherry, *Prunus avium* 'Grandiflora'.
RIGHT, BELOW The laden branches of *Prunus* 'Kanzan' hide a Turkish hazel (*Corylus colurna*).

On a fine day in June, a crowd gathers at the garden entrance. Move away, however, and you will soon find yourself alone. Where to go? A short walk will take you to the Temperate House, a wonderfully ornate Victorian glasshouse designed by Decimus Burton in 1859. The plants that grow inside it are from all the temperate areas of the world, places that experience no extremes of temperature or rainfall. They come from Asia, the Americas, Australasia and South Africa. A sign on the wall defines the collection as encompassing 'the useful, the bizarre, the common, and the highly endangered'. Step through the doors and you leave London far behind. On this sunny day, the house is dappled by the shade of trees that soar up towards the roof, and filled by the sound of running water. Look up and up again, for this is the home of the world's largest indoor plant, a Chilean wine palm (*Jubaea chilensis*). It is already 16 metres/52 feet high; what will happen when it finally outgrows the space? The path leads away from this conundrum, taking you under the sweetly scented flowers of angel's trumpet (*Brugmansia aurea*), and pushing you towards the large, soft leaves of the strawberry guava (*Psidium cattleianum*). There is information everywhere. 'Did you know', a sign reads, 'that Strawberry Guava is a serious threat to the natural habitats on all six Hawaiian Islands and elsewhere?' While we admire the tree's handsome leaves and dark red fruits, we are not allowed to forget its alter ego, the invasive weed tree that smothers all competitors. Kew's rarest plant is here too: a cycad – *Encephalartos woodii* – that is already extinct in the wild.

Cycads carry off many of the prizes at Kew. In the Palm House there is an *Encephalartos altensteinii* labelled as the oldest pot plant in Britain. It left South Africa in 1773, arrived at Kew in 1775, and was one of the first plants to be moved into the Palm House when it opened in 1848. The Palm House was principally built to display the exotic palms that were being imported into Europe in large numbers by the mid-nineteenth century. Over the years, however, the palms have been underplanted with smaller trees, climbing plants and epiphytes. Many of these tropical rainforest plants are of economic importance, many are endangered and some extinct. The hot, humid air is full of scent.

Where now? There are several other glasshouses to visit. The Princess of Wales Conservatory was opened in 1987. Where else could you experience ten different climatic environments under one roof? But Kew is not all about gardening under glass. You could go there to look at nothing but trees, and round your visit off by inspecting their canopies from the spectacular Treetop Walk. Go there in spring and you will find bluebells carpeting the woods that surround Queen Charlotte's Cottage. Go in summer, when the rose pergola is covered in flowers, or in the depths of winter, when witch hazels, flowering quinces and mahonias light up the Winter Garden.

TOP LEFT The full autumn glory of *Magnolia acuminata*.
TOP RIGHT An intensely yellow form of *Acer rubrum*,
the scarlet maple.
BOTTOM A grove of cherry trees glimpsed in autumn
over the formal hedge surrounding the Rose Garden.

Sissinghurst

The story of Sissinghurst is often told, and it has all the right ingredients to make it enduringly popular. Everybody loves a tale of transformation, and Sissinghurst was rescued from dereliction and given a new life as a house and garden of iconic beauty. Add to this a cast of forcefully unconventional and brilliantly creative characters, and you have a story that will run and run.

Vita Sackville-West and Sir Harold Nicolson bought Sissinghurst Castle, a group of ruined buildings and a sixteenth-century tower surrounded by farmland, in 1930. Vita was already an established poet and novelist by this time, and a member of what would become known as the Bloomsbury Group. Her experience at Sissinghurst later led her to write a regular gardening column for the *Observer*. Although she and Harold collaborated closely on the creation of the garden, the planting is generally attributed to Vita. Sir Harold

Nicolson, diplomat, author, critic and politician, was the garden designer. Working within an existing structure of walls and ancient buildings, he created a formal layout of long axes stopped by statues and urns, an arch or tree, and garden rooms that Vita referred to as 'a succession of privacies'. She went on to compare them to 'the rooms of an enormous house [that] would open off the arterial corridors'. This was a meaningful comparison because the Nicolsons' home was divided between several separate buildings: the main house and library, the tower where Vita wrote, their bedrooms and drawing room in South Cottage, and the Priest's House, which was their dining room. The buildings were linked by garden rooms, through which the family progressed as one might through the corridors of a house. Vita overlaid the formal bones of the garden with the voluptuous and exuberant planting for which Sissinghurst was to

LEFT The parterre beds in the White Garden are packed with a combination of white flowers and grey, green or silver leaves. Here one bed is given over to 'Iceberg' roses, another dominated by the ghostly spires of white rosebay willowherb (*Epilobium angustifolium*).
RIGHT White *Rosa mulliganii* swathes the arbour designed by Nigel Nicolson for the centre of the White Garden. A pale froth of *Ammi majus* fills the foreground.

become famous. By the time of her death in 1962, Pam Schwerdt and Sibylle Kreutzberger were already hard at work as Sissinghurst's head gardeners. They stayed on, working steadily, for nearly thirty years. In 1967 Sissinghurst was transferred to the National Trust, although the family retains the tenancy of part of the building. Sir Harold Nicolson died the following year.

By the middle of the twentieth century Sissinghurst was already becoming a blueprint for British garden design. It is probably most famous for the White Garden that Vita created in 1950 outside the Priest's House. Did you think you were tired of white gardens? Have you already seen enough of them to last a lifetime? Well, go to Sissinghurst in July and you will find something so spectacular, so wittily unexpected and inventive that you will never, ever sneer at a white garden again.

LEFT A pear tree in full bloom in the Orchard. Pheasant's-eye narcissi grow in the long grass at its feet.
RIGHT, ABOVE In the Rose Garden, the Powys Wall (named for its architect) is hidden behind a curtain of *Clematis* 'Perle d'Azur'. The bench was designed by Lutyens.
RIGHT, BELOW The soft and deliberately unstructured planting of the Rose Garden.

Enter the garden from the open space of the Orchard, for then the crowded brilliance of the design will strike you with full force. The arbour at the centre of the garden was designed by Nigel Nicolson, Harold and Vita's younger son. By mid-July it is entirely draped with the pale flowers of *Rosa mulliganii*. In its shade, a dark grey pot is planted up with black-eyed Susan, but this Susan is not the common egg-yolk yellow: she is white (*Thunbergia alata*) and her black eyes pick up the pewter colour of the pot. Clustered at her feet are white salvias (*S. x greggii* 'Alba'), artemisia's silver leaves and the tender grey stems of *Marrubium candidissimum*, and that's just the beginning of what Vita referred to as her 'grey, green and white garden'. The neat parterre beds surrounding the arbour are filled to bursting with a wonderful combination of white flowers and grey, green or silver leaves. There are white cosmos, of course, lupins and delphiniums, the everlasting sweet pea *Lathyrus latifolius* 'Albus', the astonishing, feathery fronds of *Stipa barbata*, white rosebay willowherb (*Epilobium angustifolium* 'Album'), *Ammi majus* and the white *Fuchsia* 'Hawkshead'.

On a moonlit night the White Garden must be twice illuminated, once by the moon and again by the white and silver light of leaves and flowers seen against a dark backdrop of hedges. There is an ingenious balance between the shapes and sizes of the flowers and the colours and textures of their foliage. This is the result of experience accumulated over sixty years and handed on by Vita to Pam Schwerdt and Sibylle Kreutzberger, by them to their successor Sarah Cook, and finally by her to Alexis Datta, the current head gardener. Nothing at Sissinghurst stands still for long, and although the rich and romantic nature of Vita's planting remains, many of the plants and their associations have changed over the decades in the continued effort towards improvement.

At the far end of the Rose Garden the Powys Wall, named after its architect, is entirely covered by *Clematis* 'Perle d'Azur'. Perfect pruning ensures that a densely woven fabric of purple flowers clothes the wall like a backdrop in July, turning the terrace below into a stage, and the roses in the beds below that into a riotous audience. There is a handsome Lutyens seat on the terrace, and from this viewpoint it is clear that here, once again, flagged paths and closely pruned hedges divide the space. All of the beds are seen against the backdrop of a dark hedge, an ancient wall or a lovely Kentish building. There is continuity here that underpins Sissinghurst's design, and gives the whole garden serenity.

Vita Sackville-West championed old roses, the Damasks, Mosses, Centifolias, Albas and Gallicas that still dominate the planting in the Rose Garden. In a passage from her book *In Your Garden*, she advises readers to approach them 'as though they were textiles rather than flowers. The velvet vermilion of petals, the stamens of quivering gold . . . I could go on forever, but always I should come back to the idea of embroidery and of velvet and of the damask with which some of them share their name.' The opulence of these images lives on in the Rose Garden, where much of Vita's rose collection is still intact. The planting is soft and unstructured, and the air is full of the scent of sun-warmed roses.

At Sissinghurst there is a room for every mood. Leave the cool pinks, blues and whites of the Rose Garden and go directly to the

The beds in the Cottage Garden are devoted to fiery colours all year. In spring, wallflowers and tulips dominate the show, while euphorbias provide a backdrop for *Potentilla* 'Monsieur Rouillard' and *Paeonia mlokosewitschii* or 'Molly the Witch'.

Cottage Garden beyond it, and you will be startled by a sudden onset of heat. Four yew columns stand in the centre of the garden, and around them revolves a fiery combination of marmalade-coloured heleniums, yolk-yellow achillea, yellow irises, the red *Alstroemeria* 'Princess Grace', *Hemerocallis* 'Burning Daylight' and dahlias 'Bishop of Llandaff' and 'Brandaris'.

A katsura tree (*Cercidiphyllum japonicum*) grows in one corner. In late September this fills the enclosed space with the burnt sugar scent of its turning leaves. The smell drifts through the hedge to the lovely Lime Walk, where the grey-green trunks of the trees match paving scattered with the first fallen leaves. There is still plenty to see: the final throes of the glorious Purple Border in the Top Courtyard, the Nuttery, like a green tunnel at one end of the Lime Walk, and the Herb Garden, where medicinal and culinary herbs filled the air with their scents all summer. In the Orchard, enormous autumn crocuses flower between the beehives. The trees are heavy with fruit, and Michaelmas daisies give the moat a purple fringe.

ABOVE Even as a child, Vita Sackville-West had dreamed of having her own tower, and here it is: Sissinghurst's Elizabethan Tower, where Vita had her study.
LEFT A view along the Lime Walk, with its underplanting of spring bulbs, towards the Nuttery.

Wisley

No wonder Wisley's car park is always full. It is the Royal Horticultural Society's flagship garden, a world-famous display of horticultural excellence covering 97 hectares/240 acres. The garden houses one of the largest plant collections in the world. It performs trials of ornamental and edible plants, carries out valuable scientific research in its laboratories, educates gardeners of every age from all over the world and holds several National Collections. It's no surprise that over a million people visit the garden every year.

The history of the garden begins in 1903, when Sir Thomas Hanbury donated 25 hectares/60 acres of land to the RHS. This was to form the core of the new garden of Wisley. The site had already been cultivated for twenty-five years by George Fergusson Wilson, a former treasurer of the RHS and an ambitious amateur gardener. His garden occupied the wooded area now known as the Wild Garden. Visitors come to Wisley for an intense experience of each horticultural season, and in winter they pour into the Wild Garden to see it illuminated by the eerie, snow-light cast by the National Collection of snowdrops. In spring they come to be dazzled by a medley of trilliums, primulas and epimediums that flower in the dappled shade cast by magnolias, rhododendrons and camellias.

The RHS began its planting at Wisley on a grand scale by building the Rock Garden. Such an enormous quantity of rocks was needed to cover the north-facing slope that a light railway was built to haul huge cargoes of Sussex-sandstone blocks from the road to the site. The RHS commissioned plans from Edward White, and James Pulham and Sons were engaged to realize the design. Pulham and Sons specialized in making rockeries, ferneries, follies and grottoes, and remain famous for the invention of Pulhamite, a form of artificial rock. Pulham's team worked with the sensitivity of Japanese *ishitateso*, or 'rock-setting priests', to give the garden a naturalistic appearance. They did this by ensuring that each block was orientated exactly as it had been before it was quarried. Streams and cascades were made between the rocks to run into a series of ponds at the bottom of the site. Work was completed by 1912 and the garden has been developing ever since. Today plants from every alpine region of the world thrive among the rocks. From March to April the Alpine Meadow is covered by sheets of snakeshead fritillaries, primulas, violets and *Narcissus bulbocodium*.

The scale of Wisley is best grasped from the summit of Battleston Hill, with its view down the Broad Walk and the two immense borders that line it.

RIGHT Tom Stuart-Smith's naturalistic perennial planting in curving beds that surround the lake in front of the new Glasshouse.
BELOW The Mixed Borders are designed to be viewed along the full length of the Broad Walk. Here, at the 'hotter' end of the display, the planting includes *Helenium* 'Sahin's Early Flowerer' and *Ligularia* 'Britt Marie Crawford'.

RIGHT, ABOVE The canal in the foreground of this view of the Laboratory was designed between 1969 and 1970 by Sir Geoffrey Jellicoe and Lanning Roper. Today the canal houses the largest collection in Britain of waterlilies on a single stretch of water.
RIGHT, BELOW A flowering cherry frames Henry Moore's statue *The Arch*, which stand on the summit of Battleston Hill.
PAGES 124–125 Early on an autumn morning, mist drifts across the Glasshouse Lake.

It would be natural to assume that the half-timbered building at the far end of Wisley's canal was the original house on the site. However, this is the Laboratory, purpose-built by the RHS in 1914–16 to accommodate the lecture theatre and classrooms belonging to the School of Horticulture. Sir Geoffrey Jellico and Lanning Roper collaborated in 1969 on the design of the elegant canal, where an enormous variety of water lilies grow. A much narrower strip of water runs through the small, walled garden at the canal's far end. Here plants crowd the water's edge, lush and abundant. The bright green stems of papyrus punctuate the dark water, and at the canal's far end *Thalia dealbata* displays its dusty, grey-green leaves and strange, crinkled flowers.

The mixed borders are one of the great glories of Wisley. Like so many things here, they are built on an impressively generous scale. Hornbeam hedges create the backdrop to beds nearly 130 metres/426 feet long that ascend in a great sweep towards Henry Moore's sculpture on Battleston Hill. The planting is a perfectly balanced combination of herbaceous, half-hardy bulbous plants, annuals and climbers. In midsummer, when the Mixed Borders achieve their apotheosis, the planting encompasses a spectrum that begins with cool pastel shades and gradually cranks up to the intense heat of russet heleniums, cannas, red hot poker, achillea and deep burgundy clumps of *Sedum telephium*. Many of the plants in the Mixed Borders have reached a considerable height by midsummer. Wisley's gardeners leave nothing to chance, and all of the plants are carefully staked at the beginning of the season.

The Trials Field that lies beyond Battleston Hill takes us to the intellectual heart of Wisley. Plant trials have always formed an

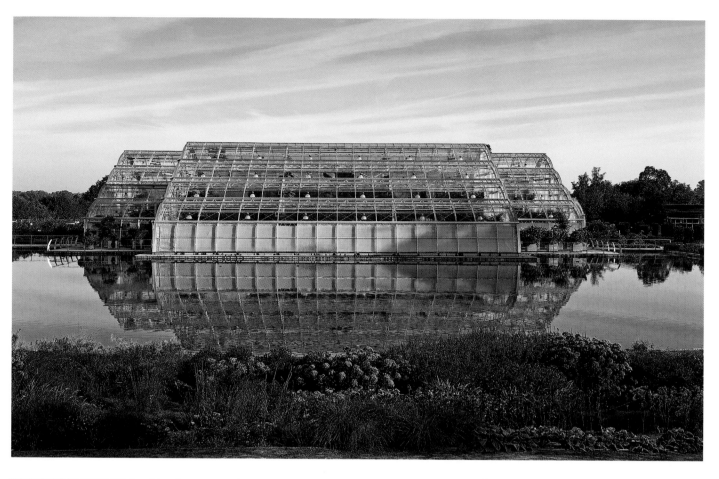

important element of the society's work, and here the process is laid bare. Every year, the field is planted with long rows made up of different kinds of delphiniums, sweet peas, dahlias, irises and pinks. These long-standing trials are carried out each year alongside one-off trials of selected plants, fruits and vegetables. The Trials Office compares the merits of the different cultivars, and gives an Award of Garden Merit (AGM) to those that are outstanding. The beauty of the trials is incidental, but it adds another layer to this fascinating area of the society's work.

An impressive new glasshouse and a lake are the latest additions to the garden. The glasshouse was opened in 2007 to mark the bicentenary of the RHS. Water laps up to the building on one side, and on the others it is surrounded by the ebb and flow of huge drifts of perennial planting that make up a new garden designed by Tom Stuart-Smith. The lake acts as a reservoir for the garden, and in late summer its banks shimmer with pale clumps of molinia and miscanthus grasses. Inside the building, the collection focuses on tender plants that visitors might grow in their own greenhouses. The building is divided into three computer-controlled climates: dry and moist, temperate and tropical. It is a horticultural theatre, where the displays of plants are changed every month.

The Eden Project

LEFT The immense curves of the Eden Project's biomes dwarf the mature trees that grow beside them.

It is autumn outside, but in the Rainforest Biome the tropical heat hits you like a body blow, deep, damp and enduring. The biome's extraordinary geodesic structure nestles against the steep side of the old china clay quarry that is the site of the Eden Project. Inside the biome the landscape is dramatically steep and undulating. Water gushes into it at roof level and flings itself, rushing and roaring, down a rocky cascade and into a pool deep among the mangrove swamps and rainforest vegetation of the Seychelles and St Helena. A canopy of outsize leaves turns the air beneath it a dusky green, and so it comes as no surprise to discover a small notice declaring 'Gigantism is a feature of island plants'. The Coco-de-Mer grows here, bearing a seed that resembles a gargantuan bottom. The entertainment value of vast leaves and suggestive fruits is high, but the intentions of Tim Smit, whose idea it was to build the Eden Project in the exhausted china clay pit north of St Austell, have always extended beyond entertainment. Eden is a charity devoted to education about sustainability, horticulture and the environment. The Rainforest Biome, like every one of Eden's astonishing structures, is designed to trumpet a message. 'You all depend on us', the rainforest plants explain, 'for food, clothes and medicine.' Everywhere you look, on the trunks of trees, in the undergrowth and on bridges, paths and walls, the messages are on the same theme. 'If we don't protect plants and the natural world, there is no sustainable future'. How much more effective this message is when theory is replaced by an experience so real and physically involving that you seem to see, touch and smell a real rainforest. Eden also plays its part in research and conservation, and it is among the island plants in the Rainforest Biome that you will find *Impatiens gordonii*, a bizzy lizzy that grows only on the Seychelles. Eden has bred its own hybrid from the *I. gordonii*, calling it *Impatiens* 'Ray of Hope.' Any money raised through plant sales is used for conservation in the Seychelles. The next area in the biome is devoted to Malaysia, where there is a house built from a patchwork of rattan mats and rusty corrugated iron. In the garden behind it is a traditional garden planted with herbs, spices, beans, taro and pak choi that grow beside the washing line where brightly coloured clothes hang limp in the damp air, and a rusting moped leans against a tree. The roar of water is deafening here. Look up, and the roof of the biome is concealed behind vegetation at the top of the waterfall. Just for a moment, you seem to be outside. The path leads steadily upwards, through West Africa to tropical South America. On the descent we return to Africa, where food crops are everywhere, coffee, palm oil, mangoes, bananas and sugar cane. So what is the situation with biofuels? Read all about

LEFT Inside the Rainforest Biome, where the dense vegetation re-creates the steamy rainforests of Malaysia, Africa and South America.
RIGHT The flowers in the foreground of this picture of the Rainforest Biome are orange canna lilies and *Crinum* x *powellii* 'Album', a white and highly scented form of the Cape lily.

LEFT, ABOVE The Prairie, where the charred timbers are a reminder that the North American prairies were partially created by controlled burning.

LEFT, BELOW A productive and highly ornamental vegetable garden surrounds the restaurant.

RIGHT The biomes sit in the crater that was once the site of a derelict china clay pit. They are surrounded by an enormous and ingeniously landscaped garden, which succeeds in combining ornamental plants with food crops from all over the world in a series of 'natural' landscapes.

it beside a brightly painted lorry stacked with sugar cane. Banana smoothie anyone? There's a convenient smoothie stall on the edge of the banana grove.

The light in the Mediterranean Biome is bright and the air dry. The plants here come from the Mediterranean zones of Europe, South Africa and California. Olive groves and vineyards may be familiar, but there is drama among the proteas, and ericas from the Fynbos area of South Africa that achieve the dimensions of small trees. The spicy leaves of pelargoniums scent the air, and in the area devoted to Little Karoo a swathe of bright pink belladonna lilies flower. The message here is the same. What cost the irrigation systems and fertilizers used to boost yields and feed the world's insatiable hunger? But Eden is a positive place. Poetry and quotations are woven in among chilling facts, and it is the project's stated aim to 'explore possible positive futures'. Smit's own attitude to negative people is well known. 'Kill them' he says, 'in the bloodiest and most public way possible'.

The extraordinary challenge of reclaiming, transforming and regenerating the derelict clay pit in 2000 was met by a team of architects, landscape architects and structural and environmental engineers, headed by Sir Nicholas Grimshaw's architectural practice. The biomes are made from frames shaped as hexagons and pentagons and covered in a revolutionary, insulating polymer membrane. The idea for the design came from a study of dragonfly wings. Given Eden's environmental stance, it's no surprise to

discover that the biomes are largely self-heating. The back wall of the Rainforest Biome serves as a gigantic storage heater, absorbing heat during the day and releasing it at night. Rainwater harvested on site is used in misting devices that drench the air, and the water feeding the cascade is recycled.

Can the Eden Project be defined as a garden? Inside the biomes the planting mimics the natural vegetation of the world's tropical and warm temperate zones. Outside, the old china clay pit was once a barren landscape, without plants or the soil to grow them in, but today the area is a richly planted garden, where generous swathes of flowering plants combine with sculptures, pleached and espaliered trees and ranks of magnificently productive vegetables that make a marvelous celebration of our own gardening tradition.

Tresco

Tresco is one of the Scillies, a group of islands almost 48 kilometres/30 miles west of Land's End in Cornwall. You can reach it by air or sea. Sea is best, for only after thirty heaving miles will you fully appreciate the island's isolation from the mainland. If the journey seems long to you now, imagine how much longer and more perilous it seemed in the nineteenth century, when visitors were already drawn to Tresco by the reputation of an extraordinary garden made by Augustus Smith, Lord Proprietor of the Scillies.

Smith took a lease of the Scilly Isles from the Duchy of Cornwall in 1834. His garden was part of a much larger project that gradually transformed both the windswept, barren island and its lawless and impoverished inhabitants. Augustus Smith was a man with big plans and the determination and energy to realize them. His methods were not always popular, but in his hands Tresco thrived; her people escaped poverty and disease and her children were educated.

Smith built Tresco Abbey, his new house, on a rocky outcrop overlooking the dunes at the southern end of the island. The garden began to evolve among the ruins of a twelfth-century abbey just below the house, and gradually expanded to fill two terraces cut from the hillside and the level area below them. Smith never intended to plant a traditional English garden on Tresco. Instead, he made use of the island's long summers, modest rainfall and mild winters to grow an ever-expanding collection of the exotic plants so fashionable in the nineteenth century. He had an advantage over his mainland contemporaries, for Scillonian sailors soon began to bring home plants for him from South America, California and Australia. He also exchanged rare seeds, plants and cuttings with William Hooker of Kew, and then with his son, Joseph. After Augustus Smith's death in 1872, the Abbey Garden continued to develop in the hands of four generations of his family. Today the 6-hectare/16-acre garden is home to a unique collection of plants and trees from the southern hemisphere, most of them too tender to survive anywhere else in Britain. The conditions on each of the garden's three levels are slightly different, the lowest level being dampest, and the top terrace hottest and driest. This has made it possible to grow plants from a range of different habitats.

It is among the ruined walls of the ancient abbey that you feel the sharp edge of Augustus Smith's determination to transform a bare, windswept hillside into a place so sheltered and sunlit that even the most tender and homesick of plants might deign to settle. Violent,

The view over the Abbey Garden from the Top Terrace. The islands of St Mary's, St Agnes and Samson can be seen on the horizon.

FAR LEFT, ABOVE In the shade of the Long Walk you can find *Cyathea medullaris*, a striking black tree fern from New Zealand.

LEFT, ABOVE, The *Aeonium* family is well represented in the garden, where its many different members have self-seeded in every crack or crevice of the walls, plants and rocky slopes.

LEFT, BELOW Agaves of all kinds also thrive on Tresco. *A. americana* 'Variegata' can be seen here growing alongside the agapanthus that self-seeds all over the garden.

RIGHT The Neptune Steps are lined with *Phoenix canariensis*, the Canary Island palm. The figure of Neptune at the top of the steps is the figurehead from a steamship wrecked on the Western Rocks in 1841.

salt-laden gales were his greatest impediment, and he began by building a 3.5-metre/12-foot wall to shelter the abbey ruins. Look uphill, and your view is stopped by the distinctive silhouettes of the Monterey cypresses (*Cupressus macrocarpa*) that he planted to baffle the wind from the north. Smith's windbreak was later reinforced with the Monterey pine (*Pinus radiata*). Ilex hedges 9 metres/30 feet high give another layer of protection inside the garden.

Augustus Smith would have strolled into his garden at the top of the slope. Today's visitors must enter at sea level, where Smith kept an ever expanding collection of figureheads taken from ships wrecked off the Scillies. It is damp down here, a dank sea garden where water stands in pools on the paths and ferns carpet the ground. The air is full of rich, northern-European woodland smells, yet the dense undergrowth is mostly made up of plants from New Zealand and the Canaries. A new frond like a tightly curled question mark springs up from the centre of *Cyanthea medullaris*, a black tree fern from New Zealand. Dappled sunlight turns the dark monkey-like fur on its stems to bronze. Then there is *Sonchus arboreus*, the Canary Islands' tree dandelion, a guinea pig's dream with flowers on stems 3 metres/10 feet high. There are camellias too, their chalk-coloured trunks cool and moist like the flanks of some unknown creature – a unicorn, perhaps. Stray from the main route on to one of many narrow, winding paths and you are in the heart of a forest, clambering over ferns that block your way, and ducking beneath a Nikau palm (*Rhopalostylis*). Before long you are bound to encounter one of many magnificent New Zealand Christmas trees (*Metrosideros excelsa*) that thrive in the damp salty air. Enormously tall, aerial roots flying in all directions, they sport bright red flowers among glossy leaves. They are the unkempt great-aunts of the garden, marvellously messy and impressive.

Sunlight and the sound of water may lure you out of the shade and into the Mediterranean Garden. Every generation has left its mark, and these stone terraces, the fountains and magnificent mosaic sheltered by a gazebo were built by Robert and Lucy Dorrien-Smith after a hurricane destroyed part of the garden in 1990. Plants don't get the freedom here that they enjoy elsewhere in the garden. They are schooled into a stricter discipline, and it is the abrupt changes of atmosphere that make this such a refreshing garden to visit. Olives clipped into tight balls, lavender and pots of golden marjoram flank the steps. Everything stands a little straighter in the sunshine, and there is a total ban on the echiums that lurch about in conversational groups, or peer nosily over hedges and walls, elsewhere in the garden.

Mike Nelhams, now garden curator, began work at the abbey as head gardener in 1983. He and Andrew Lawson, the current head gardener, have an intimate relationship with their plants. They have travelled all over the world to see them in their native habitats, and they know exactly where to place each newcomer to the garden. As one moves up from the Mediterranean Garden to the Middle Terrace, their subtle and confident style is immediately evident. Plants appear to be in control up here, and their sheer exuberant wellbeing charges the air. Someone encouraged the aeoniums to take root in the drystone retaining wall, but it was probably their idea to get so involved with the self-seeded agapanthus that flowers there, the tiny *Erigeron* daisies and the *Aloe pratensis* that seems to roam at will through the garden. The delicate, downy grey leaves of *Leucospermum conocarpum* thrust their way up through this beautiful jumble in a way that seems entirely spontaneous. Look up, and the steep slope above the terrace is covered in a tumbling carpet of cistus, aloes, magisterial agaves, groves of magnificent puyas, aeoniums of every shape and size, and sheets of the chemical-coloured flowers of *Mesembryanthemum*. Further along the terrace, where there is a summer house and a lily pool, the planting is a little more controlled. Pairs of *Agave ferox* guard a flight of steps and watsonia makes a great swathe of sunset oranges to flank the terrace. Only the echiums let the side down, for they cannot resist bending over to peer towards the sea.

A pair of *Leucadendron argenteum* stands beside the steps to the Top Terrace, their silver leaves signalling the change to even hotter, drier conditions. In the evening, when the light softens and birds flood into the garden, an extraordinary collection of plants from Australia and South Africa continue to bask in full sun. It is clear that they thrive in the dry heat and poor, free-draining soil at the garden's highest point. Gaze out from this level, and the view across the abbey ruins and the crowns of numerous palms is stopped only by the sea.

FAR LEFT Orange watsonias grow in the foreground of this view over the Middle Terrace at the heart of the Abbey Garden.
LEFT The Middle Terrace is the most sheltered part of the garden, and the planting is at its densest and most exuberant here.

139

LEFT, ABOVE Long ago the sand dunes beyond the garden were used as a garden rubbish dump, and as a result many plants, such as these agapanthus, escaped from the garden and spread all over the island.
LEFT, BELOW A view over the Mediterranean Garden and the back of the Shell House that shelters Lucy Dorrien-Smith's magnificent shell mosaic.

RIGHT, ABOVE There are many plants from the Western Cape of South Africa in the garden. In August the graceful orange flowers of *Watsonia* 'Tresco Hybrid' line the path on the Middle Terrace.

RIGHT, BELOW Tresco Abbey has been the family home ever since it was built by Augustus Smith, Lord Proprietor of the Scillies, in the nineteenth century.

Visiting the Gardens

Visit the website, telephone or e-mail all gardens for
up-to-date visiting information and opening times.

Alnwick
Denwick Lane, Alnwick NE66 1YU
Tel. 01665 511350
info@alnwickgarden.com
www.alnwickgarden.com

Beth Chatto Gardens
Elmstead Market, Colchester, Essex CO7 7DB.
Tel: 01206 822007
info@bethchatto.fsnet.co.uk
www.bethchatto.co.uk

Bodnant
Tal-y-Cafn, Nr Colwyn Bay, Conwy LL28 5RE
Tel: 01492 650460
bodnantgarden@nationaltrust.org.uk
www.bodnantgarden.co.uk

Crarae
Inveraray, Argyll, Bute & Loch Lomond PA32 8YA
Tel : 0844 4932210
crarae@nts.org.uk
www.nts.org.uk

Crathes Castle
Banchory, Aberdeen & Grampian AB31 5QJ
Tel: 0844 493 2166
crathes@nts.org.uk
www.nts.org.uk

East Ruston Old Vicarage
East Ruston, Norwich, Norfolk NR12 9HN
Tel: 01692 650432
erovoffice@btconnect.com
www.e-ruston-oldvicaragegardens.co.uk

The Eden Project
Bodelva, Cornwall, PL24 2SG.
Tel: 01726 811 911
www.edenproject.com

The Garden of Cosmic Speculation
Portrack House, Holywood, Dumfries and
Galloway, Scotland DG2 0RW
www.charlesjencks.com

Great Dixter
Northiam, Rye, East Sussex TN31 6PH
Tel: 01797 252878
office@greatdixter.co.uk
www.greatdixter.co.uk

Hidcote
Hidcote Bartrim, Chipping Campden,
Gloucestershire GL55 6LR
Tel: 01386 438333
hidcote@nationaltrust.org.uk
www.nationaltrust.org.uk

Kew Gardens
Royal Botanic Gardens, Kew, Richmond, Surrey
TW9 3AB.
Tel: 020 8332 5655
info@kew.org
www.kew.org

Levens Hall
Kendal, Cumbria LA8 0PD
Tel: 015395 60321
houseopening@levenshall.co.uk
www.levenshall.co.uk

Little Sparta
Dunsyre, Lanark, South Lanarkshire ML11 8NG
Tel: 078264956777
little_sparta@btinternet.com
www.littlesparta.co.uk

Mount Stewart
Portaferry Road, Newtownards, County Down
BT22 2AD
Tel: 028 4278 8387
mountstewart@nationaltrust.org.uk
www.nationaltrust.org.uk

Powis Castle
Welshpool, Powys SY21 8RF
Tel: 01938 551944
powiscastle@nationaltrust.org.uk
www.nationaltrust.org.uk

Scampston
Scampston Hall, Malton, North Yorkshire YO17
8NG
Tel: 01944 759111
info@scampston.co.uk
www.scampston.co.uk

Sissinghurst
Biddenden Road, Sissinghurst, Cranbrook, Kent
TN17 2AB
Tel: 01580 710701
sissinghurst@nationaltrust.org.uk
www.nationaltrust.org.uk

Stourhead
Stourton, Warminster, Wiltshire BA12 6QD
Tel: 01747 841152
stourhead@nationaltrust.org.uk
www.nationaltrust.org.uk

Tresco
Tresco, Isles of Scilly TR24 0QQ
Tel: 01720 424108
mikenelhams@tresco.co.uk
www.tresco.co.uk

Wisley
RHS Gardens Wisley, Woking, Surrey GU23 6QB
Tel: 0845 260 9000
www.rhs.org.uk/Gardens/Wisley

Numbers in **bold** refer to illustrations.

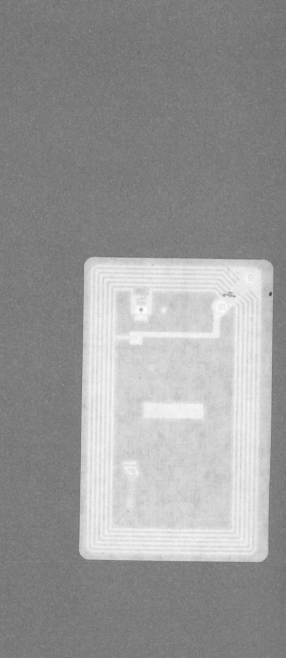